Cybersecurity Governance

A guide for executives who need to understand cybersecurity in plain, actionable language

Second Edition

Dr Darryl J Carlton

Edited by Adis Fazlic

Technics Publications
SEDONA, ARIZONA

115 Linda Vista
Sedona, AZ 86336 USA
https://www.TechnicsPub.com

Edited by Adis Fazlic

Cover design by Lorena Molinari

First Printing 2024

Copyright © 2024 by Dr Darryl J Carlton

ISBN, print ed.   9781634624749
ISBN, Kindle ed.   9781634624831
ISBN, PDF ed.   9781634624848

I dedicate this book to all those who keep fighting, learning, and applying those lessons to their day-to-day tasks. For me, the lessons of Kaizen, the Japanese philosophy of continuous learning, and improving just 1% every day are key to making progress.

I have always maintained a personal philosophy of "Do one thing every day." That might not sound very ambitious, but I found early in my career that I would go home after work and could not identify what I had achieved that day. It was very much like the Henry David Thoreau quote, "The mass of men lead lives of quiet desperation."[1]

I found great inspiration in Viktor Frankl's "Man's Search for Meaning,"[2] which is consistent with Thoreau's—it is about finding and maintaining a purpose in one's life. For me, that purpose is a constant search for knowledge, to learn more, and to be a little bit better at my job than I was yesterday.

I aim to communicate what I have learned and the knowledge I have acquired to senior executives and board members with oversight and accountability for technology in their organizations.

I am not trying to make you tech experts. My work is to support you in having an "Informed Discussion" about critical technology investments your organization is making.

If you want to play an active part in the governance and oversight of technology, then this book is dedicated to you.

---

[1] Thoreau, Henry David. *Walden—or, Life in the Woods.* Ticknor and Fields, 1854.

[2] Frankl, Viktor E. (1962). Man's Search for Meaning: An Introduction to Logotherapy. Boston: Beacon Press.

Acknowledgments

Reflecting on a career that's spanned more than fifty years, I'm awash with gratitude. A constellation of friends, family, and colleagues has guided, encouraged, and inspired me. This book is a testament to their invaluable support.

Among these guiding stars, a core group of friends stands out for their steadfastness. In recent, trying times, they've been my emotional anchors—providing laughter and solace through late-night talks, home-cooked feasts, and spontaneous get-togethers in my sanctuary of a man cave.

Wayne Bingham, a fount of ceaseless creativity, deserves special mention. His sometimes-whimsical ideas have continually nudged me out of my comfort zone, making life an ongoing adventure. His passion is nothing short of infectious.

Another pivotal figure is my lifelong comrade, Gordon Miles. His sage advice has been as treasured as the evenings we've spent unraveling the mysteries of life over his curated collection of wines.

For years, Rene and Meneja Nogueira have enveloped me in a cocoon of kindness. Their home is a hearthstone, always radiating warmth and happiness. Their friendship is a constant in an ever-changing world.

Then there's David Bowen, whose famed Chicken Kiev and his extensive range of Rum has been amazing, fueling many a late-night marathon that should have been spent writing instead of drinking.

Acknowledging the full breadth of my support network is a Herculean task, but the roll call includes Tony and Stephanie Ladias–Guy Hodgkinson, a partner in memorable dining–Siobhan McGlinchey, the queen of indulgence–Olga Carlton, and my incredible daughter Sasha, whose budding silver screen career promises to be as inspiring as her constant support has been for me.

Mike Boutel at PM-Partners has been an indispensable mentor in my professional sphere. He has provided me with a platform and a classroom to test my ideas. Our conversations have been not only cathartic but also enriching.

I extend heartfelt thanks to everyone I've collaborated with over the decades—you've been teachers, mentors, and sometimes even unwitting muses. To all the authors and scholars who've expanded my horizons, your contributions are woven into the fabric of my thoughts.

Special appreciation goes (again) to my daughter Sasha, the effervescent light of my life. Her boundless enthusiasm, along with our dog Simba, is my daily recharge, and I'm eager to see her dazzle the world soon.

To Sage and Paul, Anya and Rio. Jessica and Ricki, Olivia and Mei.

I owe an enormous debt of gratitude to Adis Fazlic, who made an extraordinary contribution to editing the content and message. While the original words were mine, the final product has been a collaboration. Adis has been with me from my PhD thesis and through various drafts of books and articles.

And last, but by no means least, Steve Hoberman of Technics Publishers. Steve and Technics published my second book, *AI Governance*. Technics is re-releasing this book with significant updates. Technics uniquely provide a platform for information technology professionals to get their voice into print.

So, thank you, one and all. You've made this journey and this book not just possible but truly meaningful.

Contents

Introduction

The world as we know it is becoming increasingly interconnected. With the advent of the "Internet of Things," our societies are inextricably linked with digital networks and systems. However, as we reap the benefits of this digital age, we also open ourselves up to new risks and challenges. Cybersecurity has, therefore, become imperative in today's digital economy. Managers must take the reins, protecting critical intellectual property and client information from cyber threats.

This book is designed to equip you with a comprehensive understanding of cybersecurity—its origins, current global context, and potential future. We'll delve into various legal frameworks and their implications on organizations, locally and globally. We will provide you, the reader, with an introduction to emerging regulations. We will provide you with a framework to both understand and critique your organization's approach to cyber governance methodologies and consequently help you shape effective compliance strategies.

What will we cover?

This book is for executives who need to understand cybersecurity in plain language. It emphasizes that as leaders, executives are responsible for having a working knowledge of cybersecurity issues affecting their organizations and the language that the experts use when discussing this subject. The introductory chapter provides an overview of cybersecurity, its history from the 1960s onwards, and why it matters today:

- **Chapter 1** covers basics like defining cybersecurity, its objectives like confidentiality and system availability, and the challenges in the field. It explains how the Internet has changed power dynamics globally.

- **Chapter 2** explores cyber threats and emerging trends, like information warfare, surveillance, and the types of risks that your organization will face. It uses examples like the Facebook Cambridge Analytica scandal to discuss appropriate responses.

- **Chapter 3** looks at the global landscape of cybersecurity, issues like intellectual property theft, and international conventions. It introduces frameworks like the Information Security Forum's Standard of Good Practice.

- **Chapter 4** examines relevant laws in the U.S. and EU. It compares the U.S. CLOUD Act and EU GDPR, highlighting potential conflicts.

- **Chapter 5** provides an overview of international agreements and conventions related to cybersecurity.

- **Chapter 6** focuses on risk assessment and management. It explores methodologies for analyzing cyber risks.

- **Chapter 7** covers cybersecurity standards and frameworks to implement for governance. It looks at ISO standards and industry best practices.

- **Chapter 8** discusses ethics in cybersecurity, emphasizing principles like privacy, integrity, responsible disclosure, and avoiding harm.

Informed Discussions

If it hasn't happened to your business already, it will!

Someone, somewhere, will hack into your systems, steal customer data, and disrupt your organization. Every 14 seconds, a business or organization is attacked—nearly 4,000 new cyberattacks happen daily.

I was in a staff meeting once when suddenly the CIO burst into the conference room and effectively screamed, "How the f*ck did this happen?" quickly followed by, "I thought we paid you guys to protect us from this sort of thing!"

Senior executives and board members are not technology experts—but as the saying goes, "The buck stops with them." When an organization is attacked, it is those with accountability for governance and oversight that the courts are holding accountable.

This book will not make you a cyber expert. This book provides business leaders with the essential information required to engage in well-informed discussions with cybersecurity experts. By arming yourself with the knowledge presented here, you will be equipped to have productive conversations about how these professionals are safeguarding your company assets. The insights presented here will enable you to understand the threat landscape and make strategic decisions alongside your technical teams to fortify company defenses. With clear communication and alignment between business objectives and security priorities, your organization can build robust protections to match the ever-evolving risks of the digital domain. Read this guide to gain the perspective needed to direct resources wisely toward strengthening your systems against those who would harm them. Knowledge and preparation are key to establishing effective partnerships between business leaders and their cybersecurity workforce. As a manager, you need to be armed with enough knowledge to assess and evaluate what is happening to your organization. You need to be armed with the language and enough background so that when someone says, "We have been hacked," you can provide effective oversight and governance for a coordinated response.

A Federal Court ruling in Australia, with respect to a large property group (Centro), found that directors were liable for misstatements in their company's financial accounts and could not rely on the advice of either managers or external advisers.

This ruling is critical. It underscores that as leaders of businesses and public sector organizations, you cannot rely on a defense of, "Our consultants said it was okay." You are required, by law, to have a reasonable understanding of those aspects of your organization over which you have management and oversight.

Informed Decisions

The requirement for directors and officers to make informed decisions is common in corporate law across almost every jurisdiction. The U.S., UK, Canada, Australia, and other countries have equivalent requirements. The law in each country knows you cannot be an expert on everything, and it doesn't ask you to be. It asks for a "reasonable" effort, showing you care about getting it right, not just done. This isn't just about ticking boxes—it's about genuine understanding and thoughtful consideration.

But the law also recognizes that you can't get bogged down in details. It asks for a balance, for the wisdom to know how deep to go without losing sight of the bigger picture. It demands responsibility without paralysis and care without over-caution.

These principles aren't just rules in a book—they echo a global understanding. From the bustling boardrooms of New York to the growing businesses in London, there's an international nod, a shared agreement that this is how leaders should lead. It's not just about following the rules—it's about embracing a way of thinking and leading that's recognized worldwide.

These laws mirror what's expected of a leader today: to be insightful, responsible, balanced, and, above all, to be someone who leads not by chance but by choice. It's about being the captain who knows the ship, the sea, and the journey ahead. That's the kind of leader the world believes in, and that's the kind of leader the law expects you to be.

When it comes to managing risk, cybersecurity is right up there. This book will help you understand cybersecurity. More importantly, it will help you ask the right questions and comprehend the answers you hear. This book will help you sort facts from fiction and make informed decisions.

About the Author

Darryl Carlton has spent 50 years working in IT. During this time, he has been an employee, a consultant, an entrepreneur, and an educator. He was the founder of a pioneering cloud business and held the first SaaS patent in the world. His experience spans large organizations, government agencies, and retailers. He earned his degrees part-time while working and raising a family, ensuring he could apply what he learned to his job. His passions are lifelong learning, reading, movies, cooking, and spending time with friends and family.

Darryl lives in Geelong (Australia) with his dog Simba. He is embarking on new adventures: packing his bags, sailing, completing a second PhD, and writing. This book is the first in a planned series aimed at the needs of managers who oversee all aspects of information technology.

www.darrylcarlton.com
darryl.carlton@me.com

About the Editor

With over two decades in manufacturing, logistics, IT systems management, and software product development, Adis Fazlic has executed in engineering, management, consulting, and director roles. This diversity of environments challenged Adis to continually examine the pivotal role of cybersecurity from various perspectives, including that of a vendor, client, private enterprise, and government agencies. These experiences, coupled with professional qualifications in science, engineering, and information technology, enable Adis to conduct rigorous independent reviews, transforming ideas into sophisticated arguments and polished content. His extensive technological and business acumen empowers authoritative assessments of texts drawing on real-world insights from diverse sectors.

In his personal life Adis loves spending time, drawing strength from his wife Almira and daughters Azra and Aleya.

Summary

This guide aims to equip executives with enough knowledge to understand cybersecurity issues, ask informed questions, and make sound decisions related to cyber risks. It covers a wide range of topics relevant to leaders seeking cybersecurity knowledge.

This book aims to empower you with the knowledge and skills necessary to provide effective governance and oversight of the cybersecurity program and responses, enabling your organization to operate safely in an increasingly complex digital world. As technology continues to evolve, the importance of cybersecurity will only grow. Our responsibility is to stay ahead of the curve, anticipate threats, and implement robust strategies to keep our organizations secure. Let's embark on this journey together. Welcome to your cybersecurity journey.

One

Understanding Cybersecurity

C ybersecurity serves as the vigilant sentinel for our computer systems and networks, guarding against threats that seek to compromise, steal, or damage our valuable digital assets. It encompasses a broad spectrum of practices and technologies designed to protect hardware, software, and data from unauthorized access, cyberattacks, and disruptions. In essence, cybersecurity ensures the integrity, confidentiality, and availability of information.

Cybersecurity's Evolution

The concept of cybersecurity has evolved significantly over the decades. Let's take a historical tour to appreciate its development:

- **1960s:** The early days of cybersecurity saw the introduction of password protection, a rudimentary yet essential measure to control access to computer systems.

- **1970s:** This era marked the advent of viruses, self-replicating programs that could spread and cause harm to computer systems. The term "computer virus" was coined to describe these malicious entities.

- **1980s:** Worms and hacking emerged as notable threats. The Morris Worm of 1988 was one of the first major Internet worms, demonstrating the potential for widespread disruption.

- **1990s:** The proliferation of the Internet led to the development and widespread use of firewalls and antivirus software. These tools became fundamental in protecting computers from external threats.

- **2000s:** The dawn of the new millennium saw the formalization of cybersecurity laws and regulations. Acts like the U.S. PATRIOT Act and the Cybersecurity Enhancement Act set legal standards and practices for protecting information systems.

Cybersecurity Today

In our interconnected world, cybersecurity is more critical than ever. It protects sensitive data, personal information, intellectual property, and the infrastructure of governments and industries from cybercriminals and malicious actors. The stakes are high, with cyberattacks posing significant economic stability, national security, and individual privacy risks.

We cannot overstate cybersecurity's importance. It underpins the trust and reliability of digital systems that power everything from banking and healthcare to transportation and communication. Without robust cybersecurity measures, the digital fabric of our society would be vulnerable to disruption and exploitation.

Cybersecurity Challenges

Despite advancements in cybersecurity technologies and practices, several challenges persist:

- **Skills Shortages:** There is a growing demand for skilled cybersecurity professionals. The rapid evolution of cyber threats necessitates continuous education and training to equip the next generation of cybersecurity experts.

- **Regulatory Issues:** Cybersecurity regulations are complex and often lag behind technological advancements. Ensuring compliance with laws that govern cyberspace requires constant vigilance and adaptation.

- **Reactive Postures:** Many organizations adopt a reactive approach to cybersecurity, addressing threats only after they have occurred. This is often due to limited resources or a lack of awareness about proactive measures.

- **Relationship Management:** As organizations increasingly rely on digital partnerships, managing the cybersecurity aspects of these relationships becomes critical. This includes vetting third-party vendors and ensuring all partners adhere to stringent cybersecurity standards.

The Path Forward

A paradigm shift from reactive to proactive cybersecurity strategies is essential to combat cyber threats. Organizations must invest in advanced threat detection and response capabilities, foster a culture of cybersecurity awareness, and collaborate with stakeholders to share threat intelligence and best practices. By addressing skills shortages through education and training programs, updating regulatory frameworks, and embracing a proactive stance, we can build a resilient digital ecosystem capable of withstanding the evolving landscape of cyber threats.

In summary, cybersecurity is the linchpin of modern digital life, safeguarding our systems and data from a myriad of threats. Its evolution from simple password protection to complex, multi-layered defenses highlights its growing significance. As we navigate the challenges ahead, a proactive and collaborative approach will be key to securing our digital future.

Compliance in Cyberspace

Leaders in the business have to balance compliance with the law and manage risks. This involves a mix of physical, administrative, and technical measures. This chapter, though, hones in on how tech can be both a blessing and a curse. Technology and the internet have shaken things up in a big way:

- **Authority** has slipped from nations to individuals, with social media playing a huge role.

- **Global power** is shifting, in particular, the U.S. no longer writes all the rules, and economic might is now increasingly coming from the East (this is important when we look into global standards and international conventions).

- **Intellectual property** and intangible assets are increasingly valuable, overshadowing physical property assets.

- **Social media** giants like Facebook and Tencent are now dominating our tech screens. In many cases, they are the delivery of news and information as well as the shopping portal.

- **Platform service providers** like Uber and Airbnb have massively changed how services are delivered, and upended the service economy.

- **Data** has become a goldmine, and **Artificial Intelligence** the miner.

To keep on the right side of the law and manage risk, organizations need to understand their regulatory environment, be aware of the risks, set their risk appetite, have a strategy to meet stakeholder expectations, and ensure everything aligns.

The point here is to do all of this effectively. Managers need to get, at least a little bit, tech-savvy. Here are some definitions to help you out:

- **Cyberspace:** is a term from the National Research Council's publication that includes all things related to computer and communication technology, the data and information these things use, handle, or process, and how all these bits and pieces connect.

- **Cybersecurity:** according to NIST (National Institute of Standards and Technology, www.nist.gov), a key organization in defining and promoting standards, cybersecurity is a multifaceted challenge that requires an arsenal of strategies. It encompasses a robust set of tools, policies, guidelines, actions, training, practices, and technologies, all aiming to fortify the virtual space in which we operate. The primary goal is to shield our digital assets against the myriad of risks lurking in cyberspace.

- **Risk:** is a measure of the threat level to an entity from potential events or circumstances. It factors in both the adverse impacts if the event occurs and the likelihood of its occurrence.

An **asset** can be data, a service provided by a system, a system capability (like processing power, communication bandwidth, or the integration of multiple systems, creating a unique and competitive capability), an item of system equipment (hardware, firmware, software, or documentation), or even a facility housing system operations and equipment. Also, there are a couple of other terms worth mentioning:

- **Information security is about preserving data's confidentiality, integrity, and availability.** It also might involve other properties like authenticity, accountability, non-repudiation, and reliability.

- **Network security:** deals with protecting networks and their services from unauthorized changes, destruction, or disclosure. It's all about ensuring the network performs its crucial functions correctly and without any harmful side effects.

In a nutshell, cybersecurity wraps up both information security and network security when it comes to electronic information. But don't forget information security also deals with physical information, like paper-based data. However, in everyday chats, cybersecurity and information security are usually used as synonyms.

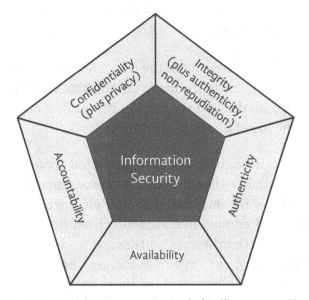

Figure 1: Essential Cybersecurity Goals (Stallings, 2019, Ch.1).

Cybersecurity Goals

- **Availability:** It's like a convenience store that's open 24/7. You want your system to be ready to roll whenever you need it.

- **Integrity:** You wouldn't want someone sneaking into your diary and adding their own entries, right? That's what integrity is all about–keeping your data from being messed with.

- **Authenticity:** This is all about making sure everyone is who they say they are, like checking IDs at a club, but for your digital world. It's about ensuring that every document is truly yours and not fabricated by others pretending to be genuine. Authenticity ensures that every person, document, and product is legitimate and credible.

- **Non-repudiation:** This is about keeping everyone honest. It's like getting a receipt when you buy something–it proves you paid, and the store can't deny selling it to you.

- **Confidentiality:** Protecting your data within the system is akin to safeguarding sensitive information within a professional environment. The integrity and confidentiality of your data are paramount, and it should not be exposed to unauthorized parties.

- **Accountability:** Every action you take within the system is akin to leaving your personal mark on a project. Your name is attached to these actions, signifying ownership and responsibility for the outcomes.

Threat versus Vulnerability

The vastness and complexity of the digital universe are manifested in the Internet, a colossal and intricate network filled with phones, computers, data centers, and a web of wires–like a massive, ever-changing maze, this sprawling ecosystem is constantly evolving, and with its evolution comes the escalating challenges we face in maintaining its security. To put this in perspective (and to provide some fun trivia), in 1969, there were four Internet hosts. By 1985, that number had grown to about 2,000. In 2023, roughly 5.3 billion hosts are connecting most of the planet.

In our ever-expanding digital world, cybersecurity is the police force guarding against vandals and criminals. Your organization's employees are vital residents, playing dual roles. They can be guardians, but in some cases, they can also be unintentional or malicious threats. Some individuals may intentionally act against the organization, accounting for 25% to 50% of cybersecurity incidents. More commonly, employees may inadvertently cause security breaches through simple mistakes, such as falling for scams or mishandling information.

Protection comes through educating employees about best cybersecurity practices, turning them into a robust first line of defense, and implementing effective controls and monitoring tools that detect and prevent internal threats without overstepping privacy boundaries. Finding the right balance between trusting employees and implementing security measures is crucial. Too much scrutiny can harm trust, while too little leaves vulnerabilities exposed.

As the working landscape changes, with remote work becoming more prevalent and laws mandating internal threat protection, new challenges in monitoring and managing internal security arise. Managing internal cybersecurity is like navigating a busy, ever-changing urban landscape. It requires a watchful eye, sound judgment, and adaptability. It's a continuous effort, reflecting the ever-changing nature of the digital world, and demands attention and investment to protect the organization effectively.

There is a subtle difference, and you will hear this in the language of your cybersecurity experts and advisors. A *threat* is anything that could harm you–like a burglar trying to break into your house. A *vulnerability* is like leaving your front door unlocked–a weakness the burglar could exploit.

Your organization needs to develop policies, procedures, and practices around both **threats** and **vulnerabilities**. Since they are different, how you mitigate these will be different.

The Battle Between User Needs and Security

People want the latest and greatest tech, easy to use, with lots of options, and it has to be secure. But the more options and easier it is to use, the harder it is to keep secure. It's like trying to keep a whole lot of beach balls underwater at the same time. The more you push down on one, another pops up, then another.

This is particularly true with the migration to cloud. We are all moving our solutions into the cloud. We have cloud vendors like Amazon, Microsoft, and Salesforce for our core applications. And there are great advantages to cloud computing. However, it also means that you are handing over, at least partially, a lot of your security management to an external provider.

Where this has become a critical issue is with small, niche solutions. Teams in your business are signing up to online cloud-hosted solutions instead of going through the IT Department. In many cases, IT has yet to learn that these solutions are being used in your organization. You, your organization, needs to know what data and business processes are operating "out in the cloud"–you have both technical and legal reasons to have visibility of what is going on and how data is being gathered, used, and secured.

You need to find a balance between meeting the needs of your business users of IT systems and meeting the security needs of the organization.

Estimating the Costs and Benefits

While it's tough to pinpoint the exact cost of a cyber breach, several research organizations have based their estimates on global averages. In conjunction with the Poneman Institute, IBM has estimated the growing cost of a single data breach to be roughly U.S.D$4.24 million, utilizing 2021 data. While it might be challenging to determine the potential cost to your specific organization, it will be significantly greater than the technology spend alone. You will suffer direct costs and far greater indirect costs such as reputational damage, impact on share price, etc. It can be very difficult to figure out how much to spend on a particular cybersecurity project when trying to ascertain what might be a reasonable Return on Investment (RoI). It's like trying to budget for car repairs—you don't know exactly what will break or when.

Looking to Best Practices and Standards for Help

Cybersecurity is about more than just protecting information—it's about protecting the business presence in the digital world. And because the digital world doesn't exist in a bubble, we need to understand where cyberattacks come from and how they affect businesses and governments alike.

Like the Toyota manufacturing system, which introduced the world to "quality is everyone's job," you cannot add cybersecurity at the end. Toyota famously eliminated the traditional "quality inspection" function at the end of the production line, where faulty cars were hammered back into something that would sell. The Toyota message was that quality had to be built in, and quality was ensured at every step along the production line. So, too, with cybersecurity, you cannot "inspect cybersecurity" into your organization and systems. Cybersecurity must be designed from the beginning to be an integral component of everything that your business does, both online and offline. Creating a cybersecurity system for a company can be a massive undertaking. It involves things like secret codes, network protocols, and malware protection. Plus, you've got to think about things like physical security, legal stuff, and staying on top of the ever-changing threat landscape. Like your commitment to quality manufacturing, you don't do cybersecurity once and say, "Okay, we have finished that project." This is something you commit to every day.

Luckily, there's already a ton of advice and standards to help. Organizations like NIST, ITU-T, ISO, and ISOC have all made guidelines to help steer us in the right direction. It's like having a cookbook to help immerse cybersecurity into your business enablement stack.

And guess what? There's more help at hand! Loads of professional and industry groups have worked hard to develop handy documents and guidelines with great advice. The top dog is the 'Standard of Good Practice for Information Security,' a mammoth 300+ page guide by the Information Security Forum (ISF). It's full to the brim with the best practices agreed upon by folks from both industry and government.

Source	Description	Date
ISF	Standard for Good Practice of Information Security	2016
ISO	ISO 27002: Code of Practice for Information Security Controls	2013
NIST	Framework for Improving Critical Infrastructure Cybersecurity	2017
CIS (Centre for Internet Security)	CIS Critical Security Controls for Effective Cyber Defence	2018
ISACA	COBIT 5 for Information Security	2012
PCI Security Standards Council	Data Security Standard v 3.2 Requirements and Assessment Procedures	2016

Table 1: International Best Practice and Standards Documents

Organizations such as the Information Systems Audit and Control Association (ISACA) and the Payment Card Industry (PCI) have also put together their own guides. It's like having a team of seasoned chefs ready to show you the best recipes for cybersecurity success!

The Militarization of Cyberspace

In the complex, interconnected world of the 21st century, the battleground has evolved, expanding from physical landscapes into the ethereal realms of cyberspace. The rise of the Internet not only revolutionized our daily lives, but forever transformed the nature of warfare and national security. This transformation has rippled globally, particularly within the United States, where the digital frontier has become a new domain of power, conflict, and influence.

From the corridors of military and geopolitical power to the bustling tech hubs of Silicon Valley, the development and deployment of cyber capabilities have emerged as both a weapon and a shield in an ever-shifting battle for information, control, and dominance. Within this intricate web of digital interactions, managers, military leaders, and policymakers navigate uncharted territories, face unprecedented challenges, and contend with ethical dilemmas.

The evolution of cyber-warfare is not merely a tale of technological advancement—it is a multifaceted narrative that intertwines with the fabric of our society, politics, commerce, and ethics. As we delve into cyber-warfare's history, progression, and implications, several key themes emerge, each shedding light on different facets of this complex phenomenon. The following exploration will illuminate the nuances of militarization, offense and defense dynamics, commercialization, ethical considerations, shifting threats, and the indispensable role of intelligence in the contemporary world of cyber warfare.

By understanding these themes, I am confident that you will gain insights into the labyrinthine nature of cybersecurity and the mounting challenges those entrusted with safeguarding our digital lives face. The journey through this landscape is enlightening and cautionary, reflecting a reality where the boundaries between war and peace, state and non-state, ethical and unethical, are constantly blurring, demanding our attention, vigilance, and wisdom.

I loved the 1983 movie "War Games," with Matthew Broderick and Ally Sheedy hacking into the U.S. Department of Defense and almost starting a global thermonuclear war. The history of cyber warfare parallels that of the Internet itself, with its beginnings in military research. The establishment of various cyber units and cyber command structures within the U.S. military underscored the Internet's increasingly critical role in offensive and defensive military operations. This militarization of cyberspace adds a significant layer of complexity to cybersecurity efforts.

Initially, cyber operations were primarily defensive, aiming to protect against external threats. However, this changed around the turn of the millennium with an increasing focus on offensive capabilities. This shift is particularly significant for cybersecurity leadership as it requires different tactics and strategies.

The growth of the cyber warfare industry has led to the rise of private firms that develop and sell offensive capabilities. This commercialization poses additional challenges as it means that powerful tools and techniques can and increasingly do fall into the hands of malicious actors.

The stockpiling of software vulnerabilities (zero-day exploits) by governments for use in offensive operations raises serious ethical and security concerns. While these exploits could provide an advantage in cyber warfare, they also pose a threat to critical infrastructure and general computer users. The ethical implications of this practice have yet to be fully addressed and resolved.

While this book is essentially a guide for business leaders, I am discussing military applications for a couple of reasons:

In 2016, a set of tools was "misplaced" by the U.S. National Security Agency (NSA). These tools were created under the auspices of a defensive capability known by the acronym "NOBUS" (Nobody But Us). These tools were then auctioned off on the dark web by a group called The Shadow Brokers. Civilian hackers and "unfriendly governments" now have the same level of sophistication as the most secret of the U.S.'s three letter agencies.[3]

Second, whatever can be created by government hackers can be developed in the shadow world of hacking.

---

3 NSA = No Such Agency.

The countries involved in cyber warfare have evolved over time, with a focus shifting toward major powers like China, Russia, and the U.S. and volatile regions such as North and South Korea. This shift necessitates constant re-evaluation and adaptation of cybersecurity strategies.

While the concept of cyber-warfare often brings to mind the notion of attacks and defenses, intelligence gathering remains a fundamental aspect of cyber operations. The ability to gather, analyze, and act upon information in cyberspace is integral to national security.

In light of these developments, cybersecurity leadership must remain adaptable and forward-thinking. They must not only respond to current threats but also anticipate future challenges in the evolving landscape of cyber warfare. They must also navigate the complex ethical issues raised by practices, such as stockpiling software vulnerabilities and using them for offensive operations.

Lex Informatica

The concept of 'Lex Informatica' is an analogy to the 'Lex Mercatoria' of the Middle Ages. It suggests that just as merchants of the Middle Ages needed a common set of rules to facilitate international trade, in the modern digital era, we need a universally agreed-upon set of rules or norms to regulate digital interactions that cross international borders.

These norms would be expected to govern a variety of areas within the digital landscape, including, but not limited to, e-commerce, digital communication, social media interactions, data privacy and protection, and digital rights. They would also ideally address more complex issues like cybercrime and cyber warfare.

Establishing this framework, however, presents a multitude of challenges. Countries and cultures have diverse perspectives on data privacy, Internet censorship, and digital rights, making consensus difficult to achieve. Moreover, enforcing such norms in the international digital landscape is another challenge, given the anonymity and borderless nature of the Internet.

The 'Lex Informatica' concept points towards the necessity of international cooperation, the involvement of both public and private sectors, and a collective effort to shape a secure and fair digital future. It underscores the critical role of cybersecurity leadership in navigating these complex issues and driving the development of such norms.

Just as 'Lex Mercatori' provided a set of agreed-upon rules for international trade, the 'Lex Informatica 'is a consensus-driven framework for governing digital interactions.

We will elaborate on some of the U.S. CLOUD Act's concerns and contrast that with the EU's GDPR. Building on this, Chapters Four and Five will further examine the specific challenges posed by each regulation. In Chapter 5, we will go into more detail about international conventions.

A Framework for Global Leadership

In the vast and intricate digital landscape of the 21st century, traditional boundaries and norms are continuously challenged and redefined. As the cyber domain grows, it ushers in a new era of complexity, presenting challenges across legal, cultural, political, and technological fronts. From crafting global cyber norms that resonate with diverse cultures to transforming defense strategies, the intersection of public and private spheres, and reimagining international relations, the stakes are high, and the solutions are elusive.

The following exploration sheds light on the fundamental issues underlying this digital transformation. It delves into the pressing need for a shared understanding of conduct in the global digital space, the unprecedented role of tech giants, the redefinition of sovereignty, the intricacies of enforcing cyber laws, and the evolving dynamics of defense, law enforcement, and international relations in cyberspace.

This examination goes well beyond the limitations of an academic exercise—it is a call to action for leaders in business, government, and beyond. In a world where the traditional lines of power and control are blurred, and where threats emerge from nation-states and non-state actors, there is an urgent need for vision, understanding, and adaptive strategies. The challenges are multifaceted, and the solutions must be equally complex and nuanced.

This book aims to equip leaders with insights to navigate the evolving paradigm of cyber governance. By arming yourself with this knowledge, you will be better prepared to adapt and make strategic decisions in a landscape of constant change. The perspectives provided will enable you to shape your path forward and maintain authority even as threats and regulations shift. With this practical guidance, you can turn uncertainty into an advantage and confidently navigate emerging cyber challenges.

A significant challenge is developing and applying global cyber norms. Just as international trade in the Middle Ages needed a shared understanding of conduct, so too does the global digital space. This is complicated by the vast array of different national laws, cultural practices, and societal norms that exist across the world. Formulating a set of globally agreed-upon digital norms is an enormous task (see Chapters 4 and 5).

Social media giants and other tech companies play an outsized role in the digital space, often acting as regulators of behavior on their platforms. As private sector entities, they are instrumental in shaping digital norms and can be key partners in developing new standards for cyberspace conduct.

Traditionally, sovereignty has been tied to physical geography, with states having authority over their territories and citizens. The digital realm disrupts this notion, as data and online activities don't adhere to physical boundaries. Thus, redefining sovereignty in the age of cyberspace presents a significant challenge.

Once digital norms are agreed upon and codified into law, the challenge of enforcing them arises. The enforcement of these laws is far more complex in the digital realm than in the physical world due to the anonymous and transnational nature of cyber activities.

As cyber threats increasingly become part of national security concerns, defense and law enforcement agencies must adapt their strategies and capabilities. This transformation involves not only technological changes but also changes in mindset, policy, and legal structures.

In the old global order, failed international relationships could result in war, sanctions, and trade embargoes. In the digital age, the dynamics of international relations are more complex and less predictable. Cyberattacks, information warfare, and digital espionage all necessitate a rethink of international relations and diplomacy.

Understanding these challenges is crucial for private and public sector leaders. It requires a comprehensive grasp of technology, international relations, law, and a vision for the future of digital interactions.

In a Nutshell

In this first chapter, I have attempted to make the point about how the traditional power dynamics of nation-states have been disrupted in cyberspace. Cyberattacks, data thefts, and other digital threats have not just come from other nations but increasingly from non-state actors, including individuals and corporate entities.

These actors, or more often groups of actors, can operate independently or as proxies for nation-states, creating a new level of complexity and unpredictability in the cyber landscape. These changes fundamentally challenge the conventional vertical and horizontal structures of power and control, as established in the pre-digital era.

This chapter also points out that existing legal and regulatory frameworks are ill-equipped to manage this new 'disorder effectively' (much more on this topic in Chapters 4 and 5).

I have then identified key challenges to be aware of and manage in this new paradigm of increased cybersecurity threats. These are indeed critical issues to address to develop effective and responsive strategies for cyber governance.

There is an urgent need for ongoing conversation and proactive action to navigate the cyber landscape. As a leader in business or government, it is critically important that you develop a working understanding of the shifting dynamics of power and control in cyberspace and the necessity of studying and updating our approaches to cybersecurity and cyber law.

The next chapter on Threats and Trends will dive into these challenges.

The digital world has reshaped the power dynamics from the world stage to individual levels. This journey has shown us the new challenges that have emerged and why it's so important to study cybersecurity and cyber law. Now, let's get the conversation going and see how it applies to your organization.

Key Messages

- Cybersecurity protects computer systems, networks, hardware, software, and data from theft, damage, and disruption. It has evolved from early password protection to combating modern threats like malware, hacking, and ransomware.

- Cybersecurity matters because it safeguards sensitive data, intellectual property, business systems, and critical infrastructure from criminals and malicious actors. Successful attacks can be hugely costly.

- Balancing usability and security is an ongoing challenge, as more user-friendly systems tend to have more vulnerabilities. Employees can also be both guardians and threats when it comes to cybersecurity.

- Many organizations offer frameworks, standards, and best practices for cybersecurity, guiding strategy, controls, governance, and risk management. Staying up-to-date is crucial.

- The militarization and commercialization of cyberspace have led to increasingly sophisticated state and non-state threats, requiring agile defense. Offensive cyber capabilities raise ethical dilemmas.

- Achieving global norms and rules to govern cyberspace is complex but critical. Public-private cooperation, rethinking sovereignty, and transforming law enforcement are key challenges.

- Cybersecurity leadership today requires understanding the multifaceted landscape, embracing public-private collaboration, and having a vision to shape a secure digital future.

Two

Threats and Trends

The Law Council of Australia was right on the money when they said, "Cybercrime is a large problem that every business must deal with." Cybersecurity incidents, from hacking to data leaks, are becoming daily news.

No company is immune, not even industry giants like Dropbox, Yahoo, eBay, Sony, or Apple. When such big players become cybercrime victims, millions (possibly billions) of customer details are often at risk. And it's not just the sheer size of these breaches that is alarming–it's their increasing frequency and sophistication.

Let's be clear: cybercrime and cybersecurity aren't just buzzwords. They're serious issues affecting everyone online. As a business leader, you hold personal and commercially sensitive information about your clients. A cyberattack could have devastating consequences for your customers and business–at minimum, you face reputational damage. However, more than likely, there will be direct loss as well as the cost of repair and future prevention.

Without exaggerating the problem, it's important to know that cybercrime is now one of the top concerns of the global economy.

The Internet and advancing technology have transformed every aspect of our lives. And with this comes an evolving threat landscape, not just for nation-states but also for businesses and individuals. In response, attitudes and behaviors have shifted from harmless hacker pranks to serious, organized crime and state-led cyberattacks.

As a leader of a business or government organization, you want to understand how technology continues to influence human behavior and the implications this has for your role.

This chapter provides an overview of the threats and trends emerging from the interconnected world and the growth of cyberspace, of which the World Wide Web (which we often think of as the Internet) is just one part. Understanding recent events can help shape our strategy moving forward. We all need to know more about cybersecurity and its impact on our workplace and personal lives. This book is for everyone who interacts with cyber professionals in any capacity. It is not trying to make you a technical expert. Instead, the purpose is to allow you to converse with technical experts, understand what they say, and make informed decisions. We encourage you to apply forward-thinking logic and risk management to future scenarios.

Here's a breakdown of what we'll cover:

- **Context:** We'll explore the threats and trends that have emerged as the Internet has evolved to become an essential and integrated component in our lives. This integration has led directly to the rise of cyber risks, and we will look at how these concepts have evolved in the digital age to become the threats we are now facing.

- **Global Risk:** We'll take a look at the global impact of these threats and trends.

- **The Action Imperative:** Just like "quality is everyone's job," so is cybersecurity. Threat actors are not just targeting nation-states. This gets personal as it affects us, our customers, our businesses, and the government agencies providing services. We all need to be aware of our role and contribution to protect our data and systems.

As we navigate the threats of cybersecurity, there are six key lessons to keep in mind:

1. Most software is not well-written and lacks security.

2. When the Internet was first built, it had just four hosts. Security was never the "prime directive" in its initial design—it was about exchanging information freely between research organizations. The Internet has no central control—no one place where you can "flick the switch." This lack of centralized control has become its greatest power (it cannot be turned off) and, at the same time, has opened the entire connected world to risk.

3. Computerized systems can be used against us due to their flexibility and extensibility.

4. The flexibility and resilience that "no central controlling point" gives to the Internet also increases the inherent complexity, which also means it's easier to attack than defend.

5. The Internet's ongoing evolution, including hardware and software component changes, continuously introduces new vulnerabilities. These vulnerabilities emerge when systems interconnect.

6. Getting online, connecting, and subscribing to new services is becoming easier. Anyone in your organization can subscribe to some software online (and probably does). This also means that attacks are always improving and becoming easier, faster, and cheaper—and have a far greater impact against an exponentially connected world.

In a nutshell, we're all in the fast-evolving landscape of cybersecurity. Understanding the threats and challenges we face is the first step in better protecting our clients and businesses. Let's delve deeper.

Major Cybersecurity Threats

Let's take a moment to explore some of the different types of cyber threats your business, workplace, or service provider might encounter. Even though the terms might seem just a little bit techie, please understand these can be essential to your cybersecurity strategy:

- **Malware:** Malware, or malicious software, is a program created to harm or disrupt a computer system. It's often sneaked into your system through legitimate-looking software, email attachments, or while browsing the web. Once installed, it's hard to detect and remove.

- **Phishing:** This is a ploy where fraudsters trick you into revealing sensitive information like passwords. Imagine getting an email that seems to be from your bank. The email directs you to a website that looks just like your bank's site. If you enter your login details there, bam! The fraudsters have what they want: a door into your private world.

- **Ransomware:** This is a type of malware that locks you out of your system or data. You'll only regain access after paying a ransom to the attacker. This threat is popular because of its potential to extract money directly from both businesses and individuals. A recent survey of law firms being held to ransom suggested that most will pay to stop further attacks from occurring and to keep the fact that they were attacked quiet.

- **Web Seeding Techniques:** Also known as 'malvertising,' this technique exploits vulnerabilities in frequently visited websites. The attackers hack these websites to deliver malware through ads and downloads.

- **DDoS Attacks:** Distributed Denial of Services (DDoS) attacks might not be common for smaller entities, but they can still impact you. In a DDoS attack, a service you and your customer use heavily and depend upon (like your website or email) is overloaded with requests, causing it to crash. This often has a domino effect on smaller associated entities.

- **Microsoft Office Macro Infections:** Cybercriminals often use Microsoft Office macros, small programs running in Office applications, to infect computers. Opening a document with an infected macro can potentially compromise your system.

- **Identity theft:** Criminals steal personal information like Social Security Numbers and driver's license details, then impersonate their victims to gain access to sensitive data or make fraudulent purchases using the victim's identity.

- **Man-in-the-Middle Attacks:** The attacker secretly inserts themselves into a two-party transaction, intercepting communications between the parties and relaying messages in order to eavesdrop, steal data, or alter interactions without the main parties' knowledge.

- **SQL Injection:** Malicious code is surreptitiously inserted into database search boxes or fields to get access to, steal, delete, or corrupt sensitive data held within the database.

- **Zero-Day Exploits:** Newly discovered software security vulnerabilities that attackers can use to adversely affect and compromise computer programs and systems before vendors have time to address them with patches and fixes.

- **IoT Attacks:** The lack of basic security features in many Internet of Things devices like smart home tech can allow them to be hijacked and used for distributed denial of service (DDoS) attacks or to spy on users.

- **Supply Chain Attacks:** By compromising a software company within the supply chain, attackers can embed malicious code or components into software updates or installers that subsequently infect the company's clients and customers.

- **The Enemy Within:** Current or former employees, contractors, or business associates who misuse their authorized access to networks and systems intentionally or unintentionally to sabotage, steal data, or harm the organization.

- **Social Engineering:** In the context of cybersecurity, refers to a method of manipulation that exploits human psychology rather than technical hacking techniques. It involves tricking or deceiving individuals into divulging confidential or personal information, such as passwords or bank account numbers, which can then be used for fraudulent or malicious purposes. This is often the most prevalent form of cybersecurity breach perpetrated against individuals.

- **Rogue Access Points:** Setting up compromised wireless routers or WiFi access points to intercept wireless traffic from victim devices and siphon sensitive data off the network.

It might sound daunting, but knowing what you're up against is the first step to enhancing your security. Now, let's look at how to stay one step ahead of these threats.

Over the next couple of pages, we will dig deeper into the modern cyber landscape. Just as explorers of old needed maps and compasses, our tools are knowledge and understanding in the world of the Internet and cyberspace. We will unpack key concepts that, while they might sound familiar, play different roles in the digital world.

You see, technology has rewritten the rules in many ways. It's like someone came along and shook the whole world like a snow globe–stirring up changes in geography, economy, and politics. This great shake-up has led to an array of challenges that we must now navigate:

- **Information Warfare:** In the context of modern digital conflicts, malware is like a newly developed type of ammunition, increasingly used with malicious intentions to disrupt systems and halt operations. This forms a part of the larger concept of information warfare, where information is both a weapon and a shield, utilized strategically to gain the upper hand against an opponent. This involves safeguarding one's own information resources while exploiting or sabotaging the information assets of the adversaries. While malware serves as a potent tool in information warfare, it is also employed in other domains, such as cybercrime, espionage, and hacktivism, highlighting the diverging scopes of these intertwined yet separate concepts.

- **Cyber Espionage:** Even spies had to work from home during COVID (not really, but it sure seems that way). Digital spying is the reality in our interconnected world. We can be spied upon from a distance, without James Bond peering through our windows (I liked Sean Connery best). Cyber espionage by nation-states, competitors, and criminal groups poses a growing threat, seeking to steal sensitive data and intellectual property for strategic advantage. Businesses must adopt vigilant cybersecurity measures, like encryption and secure networks, to safeguard against potential espionage attempts. Staying informed on the latest cyber espionage threats allows more effective protection.

- **Surveillance:** Sometimes connected with Cyber Espionage, increased monitoring in the digital space might sound a bit Big Brother-ish, but it's part of our new reality. Recently, we read about a business installing key-stroke monitoring software on WFH employees' devices to monitor their activity. This is a form of surveillance, and malicious hacking might install this type of worm on a device to surveil the user's activity.

- **Privacy Threats:** With the digital world comes digital threats. This includes data breaches and sharing, face and voice recognition technology, the fusion of tech and humanity, advanced analytics, big data, and even psychological profiling.

- **Critical Infrastructure Risks:**[4] Our essential services depend more on technology than ever before, making them more vulnerable to digital threats. While some of the examples and associated risks sound like the plot of a Hollywood movie, they are very real:

  o **Power grid attacks:** Hackers could access control systems and cause blackouts by shutting down power plants. The Ukraine power grid was subject to cyberattacks in 2015 and 2016.

  o **Transportation disruption:** Railway signaling, air traffic control, and shipping port operations are vulnerable to interference or shutdown via cyberattacks.

  o **Financial systems hacking:** Major banks and financial markets rely on networks vulnerable to attacks that could have systemic economic impacts.

  o **Telecommunication network disruption:** Denial-of-service attacks (discussed earlier) can shut down communications systems

---

[4] for example, the "Security of Critical Infrastructure Act 2018."

like phone networks and Internet
infrastructure.

o **Water treatment hacking:** The control
systems for water treatment plants and
distribution could be altered to impact
water supplies or safety.

o **Healthcare system compromise:** Malware
infections at hospitals have disrupted
operations, putting patients at potential
risk. Medical devices could also be
vulnerable.

o **Oil and natural gas infrastructure:**
Pipelines, refineries, and drilling platforms
increasingly rely on digital systems that
could be hacked to cause physical failures.

o **Dams and flood control manipulation:**
Outdated systems controlling dams and
flood barriers could be breached to trigger
catastrophic flooding.

o **Chemical industry cyber threats:**
Manufacturing plants with hazardous
materials have been targeted to potentially
cause chemical spills or leaks.

• **Information Integrity Risks:** Trusting the truth
and reliability of information is becoming more
challenging. The obvious examples are the
manipulation of digital photography and "deep
fakes." In the not-so-distant past, a photograph was

proof of a standard acceptable in court. Not so much anymore. Just look at the 'deep fakes 'of politicians, celebrities, and other public figures. These fakes now include copying their voice to make them appear to be saying things they did not.

- **Data Prevalence:** The shift to the cloud means that the physical boundaries of your network (the file cabinet in your office) are disappearing and security measures must evolve to protect information wherever it's accessed. The 'walls' of your office no longer provide a barrier, so you need new ways to ensure that only authorized individuals can access your files. This requires a more complex approach to authentication, encryption, and monitoring.

- **Internet of Things (IoT):** The explosion in interconnected devices means more potential points of entry for security threats. Your refrigerator is now talking to the supermarket. The toilet you buy in the future might be talking to your doctor behind your back. And your bathroom scales may not be inclined to keep your secrets.

In the "good old days" (before the year 2000), it was mostly governments that had to worry about national security and protecting businesses. Well, with changes in power and relationships, businesses find themselves increasingly under threat. And frustratingly, they're often legally restricted in how they can defend themselves.

The Internet is a driving force behind these shifts in power and relationships. It's made it possible for even groups of individuals to potentially threaten governments.

Think about how malware is being used as a weapon. A recent example was a cyber operation known as Cloudhopper. In 2017, BAE Systems and PricewaterhouseCoopers identified this significant cyberattack campaign. The operation primarily focused on infiltrating IT and cloud service providers, including major firms like IBM and Hewlett Packard Enterprise, to access their client's data and networks. This marked a strategic shift in tactics, with state-sponsored groups launching sophisticated supply chain attacks that represented an advanced persistent threat capable of avoiding detection for several years.

We've entered an era where everyone is eavesdropping on everyone else. Governments, corporations, militaries, law enforcement, intelligence agencies, hackers, criminals, terrorists–the list goes on. With our world becoming more complex, the need for real-time intelligence has never been greater. This, alongside the fact that the Internet and cyber technology have made it so easy to exploit intellectual property and other valuable information, has led to a rise in surveillance and espionage.

This might sound daunting, but you can confidently navigate this landscape with the right knowledge and understanding. This chapter is your compass–helping you understand the terrain and stay on the right path.

The Facebook/Cambridge Analytica Scandal

In early 2018, Facebook was embroiled in a significant data breach scandal involving the political data firm, Cambridge Analytica. The controversy began when it was discovered that Cambridge Analytica had improperly obtained personal data from over 87 million Facebook users through an external app in 2015. This mishandling of information led to Facebook's CEO being questioned by Congress and being fined in both the U.S. and UK.

The issue might have been averted as early as September 2015, when Facebook employees were reportedly aware of Cambridge Analytica's practices. Cambridge Analytica harvested this information through a seemingly harmless personality quiz, pulling data not only from participants but also from their friends, leading to a massive accumulation of information. This data was later employed in political campaigns, including Donald Trump's 2016 presidential campaign and the Brexit Leave campaign.

A whistleblower, Christopher Wylie, came forward in March 2018, shedding light on Cambridge Analytica's actions and quoting, "We exploited Facebook to harvest millions of people's profiles. And built models to exploit what we knew about them and target their inner demons." Despite allegations, Facebook contested the narrative that the information was taken without consent and continued to deny giving Cambridge Analytica data even after the fine.

Further complications arose from potential Russian connections and the apparent failure of Facebook to ensure that all harvested data had been deleted. This resulted in suspensions and ongoing debates about data integrity and responsibility.

In conclusion, the Cambridge Analytica scandal exposed significant lapses in data protection practices, resulting in financial and reputational damage to Facebook. It serves as a stark reminder of the importance of responsible data handling and timely response to red flags. The incident highlights the complexity of modern data management and the ethical considerations that companies must navigate in our increasingly interconnected digital landscape.

Internet of Things (IoT)

As mentioned, the Internet of Things (IoT) is dramatically changing our lives. The ability for devices to communicate amongst themselves and between systems opens up limitless opportunities. Airplanes in flight can perform automated diagnostics and communicate with supply chain systems to order parts and deliver them to their destination airport. Our phones talk to our cars. Smart locks are connected to your phone or smartwatch and know when you arrive home, unlocking the front door before you get there. However, these benefits are not without risks. The same connectedness that allows for increased efficiency and convenience also creates potential vulnerabilities for data and privacy breaches.

This presents a significant challenge, not only to non-technical executives and staff, but also to security professionals, lawmakers, and individuals alike. To protect the vast array of government, business, and personal information, privacy, and identity in the era of IoT, we need to do the following:

- **Educate Ourselves:** Knowledge is power, as they say. Understanding the basics of how your work or personal IoT devices work, what data they collect, and how that data is used can help make informed decisions about which devices to use and how to use them securely.

- **Secure our Devices:** Many IoT devices come with default usernames and passwords that are easy for hackers to guess. Changing these default credentials and regularly updating passwords is important to reduce the risk of unauthorized access. Additionally, keeping device software up-to-date can help protect against known vulnerabilities.

- **Be Mindful of Data Sharing:** Many IoT devices and apps share data with third parties. Read privacy policies and terms of service to understand what data is being collected and who it is being shared with. Adjust privacy settings to limit data sharing where possible.

- **Implement a Secure Network:** Use a secure network for IoT devices. In your work environment, ensure that your expert teams have taken steps to deploy IoT devices only on networks that they know are secure and that they can demonstrate the security measures taken. In your personal life, at home, for example, make sure that your Internet router has a secure password—you must change the manufacturer's default Admin settings. Use a firewall. Disable remote network management unless you need to access your network when you are not home. Create a Guest Network and password that are different from your family connections. Disable SSID Broadcasting so your home network is invisible to anyone scanning for a connection. If you can, you might consider a separate home network designated for these connected IoT devices to isolate them from computers and smartphones that contain sensitive information.

- **Regulation and Compliance:** Lawmakers and regulators have a role to play in ensuring IoT device manufacturers are held accountable for the security of their products. New laws may be required to protect consumers and their data. Moreover, organizations must comply with data protection laws, especially when dealing with sensitive user data.

- **Consider the Need versus Risk:** Before purchasing an IoT device, consider whether its convenience outweighs the potential security risks. For instance, a smart refrigerator may be convenient, but it could also provide an access point into your network for a potential attacker.

The IoT era is still relatively new, and as technology advances, so will the challenges we face. However, we can mitigate these risks and safely navigate this interconnected world with proper education, precautions, and legislation.

Growing Global Risk

As the digital landscape rapidly evolves, our adaptability as leaders in our industry becomes paramount. We're amid a global power shift, with nations like China ascending, as witnessed in initiatives like One Belt, One Road. Our organizational and business response to these changes must be agile, recognizing and leveraging the geopolitical and business transformation driven largely by digital technologies.

Moreover, the democratization of information, fueled by personal technology like smartphones, has realigned power from nations to individuals. This significant change impacts social dynamics and necessitates an adaptive approach to our business strategies. We must empower our stakeholders and align them with this shift.

An equally critical transformation is the value migration from physical to intangible assets. Our intellectual property, including data like customer preferences and purchasing history, product designs, and business processes, now outweighs our physical assets. This reality emphasizes our need to protect and harness our digital resources. Our innovative ideas and proprietary knowledge are essential for sustaining our market advantage.

Data is indeed our modern gold. Its misuse can lead to grave consequences, as seen in incidents like Petya and NotPetya, which we discuss in Chapter 3. Secure handling of our data must be at the forefront of our strategic considerations, mitigating all potential risks.

In parallel, the balance between privacy and surveillance is a tightrope we must traverse with precision. We have an ethical and business imperative to protect the data privacy of our stakeholders while capitalizing on data-driven growth opportunities.

Shifting from information management to data governance, we bear additional responsibilities. Complying with regulations and managing substantial information requires strong leadership and a focused approach.

Cybersecurity is a priority we cannot afford to neglect. The threats are real and constantly evolving. Our defenses must be robust, and our teams well-equipped to handle potential challenges.

In response to these trends, some key strategies and actions need to be considered:

- **Working Together Across Borders:** Just like the Internet connects everyone globally, people and governments should also come together to decide the rules for using the Internet. This can include protecting creative ideas (like movies, music, or inventions), how businesses use and protect customer data, and how to prevent cybercrimes. This collaboration is essential because the Internet doesn't belong to one country: it's global.

- **Businesses Need to Step Up:** All businesses today use the Internet and constantly collect more and more customer data. So, they need to take Internet-related risks seriously. This means they must keep customer data safe, follow Internet-related laws (in their operating areas), and take an active role in making the Internet safer.

- **Learning About the Internet:** Everyone, from ordinary people to leaders in government and business, needs to understand the Internet better. This can include knowing your online rights, the ethical rules of using new technology, and how companies use and protect your data. By understanding these things, people can make better decisions about using the Internet and technology.

- **Finding a Balance Between Safety and Privacy:** On one hand, the Internet needs to be safe. On the other hand, people have a right to privacy. This balance is tricky to achieve. It requires open conversations between people, companies, and governments. Solutions could include laws that protect privacy, technology that keeps data secure, and companies being more open about how they use and protect customer data.

- **Being Open to Change:** The Internet and technology are always changing. So, our rules, security measures, and strategies must also change with time. This requires continuous learning, trying out new ideas, and being ready to adapt.

Overall, while using the Internet and technology comes with risks, it also brings many opportunities like new ways of communicating, easier access to information, and more efficient ways of working. If we all work together, we can enjoy these benefits in a safe and fair way.

In a Nutshell

In Chapter 2, we looked closely at the current dangers in the online world. We focused on the growing number of cybercrimes, how these threats constantly change, and the need for smart planning and protection in today's digital age.

The chapter breaks down various online threats that could harm computers and data. This includes malware (harmful software), phishing (tricking people into revealing personal information), ransomware (locking files until a ransom is paid), and other methods used by criminals. We also highlighted a number of important lessons about why computers are often easy to attack, mainly because of poorly written software and the complexity of systems and business processes that those systems support.

One significant example we examined was the scandal involving Facebook and Cambridge Analytica, where personal data from millions of Facebook users was misused. We used this example to stress the importance of keeping data safe and handling it responsibly.

We also discussed the Internet of Things (IoT), which refers to the connection of everyday devices like refrigerators and thermostats to the Internet. While this technology offers exciting possibilities, it also brings risks of privacy breaches. We provided some practical tips to keep information safe, especially in this new era of connected devices.

Towards the end, we looked at the growing risks on a global scale due to our ever-connected world. We called for teamwork across countries, leadership within businesses, and a balanced approach to safety and privacy. We emphasized that cybersecurity isn't just a technical issue—it's something that affects us all and needs strong action.

We talked about the increasing number and severity of cyber incidents and explored the complex challenges we face today. We emphasized that no individual or company is safe from these online threats, and we all need to recognize how serious this issue is.

Key Messages

- Cybercrime and cybersecurity threats are serious issues affecting everyone online, not just buzzwords. Cyberattacks can have devastating consequences.

- Major data breaches at large companies show no one is immune to cyberattacks. The frequency of attacks is also increasing.

- Cybercrime is now one of the top global economic risks. Leaders must understand the evolving threat landscape.

- The Internet and advancing technology lead to new cyber risks like information warfare, surveillance, critical infrastructure threats, data integrity issues, etc.

- Everyone has a role in cybersecurity—it's not just up to governments anymore. Businesses must step up and individuals need awareness.

- Software vulnerabilities, the open nature of the Internet, system interconnectedness, and complexity make cyberattacks easier than defense.

- Cyber threats are always evolving and becoming more sophisticated. Continuous learning and adaptation are crucial.

- Recent incidents like Facebook/Cambridge Analytica scandal show lapses in data protection can cause major financial and reputation damage.

- Internet of Things expands convenience but introduces cyber risks. Users need education on securing devices and networks.

- As digital transformation accelerates, businesses must be agile and protect intellectual property and customer data.

- Public-private cooperation is essential for tackling global cyber risks. Openness, flexibility, and the right safety/privacy balance are key.

Three

The Global Landscape

We exist and operate in a globalized world, in terms of trade, tourism, geopolitics, and the interests of corporations and nation-states. How public and private organizations respond to cyberattacks is becoming increasingly important. When dealing with a cyber threat or an ongoing attack, decision-makers need to assess and anticipate likely reactions. Let's delve into some examples of past cyber-related activities that emphasize the significance of cybersecurity and geopolitics:

- **Stuxnet:** Perhaps one of the most famous cyberattacks in history, the Stuxnet worm, was discovered in 2010. It was specifically designed to target Iran's nuclear infrastructure, disrupting its uranium enrichment process. The attack was widely attributed to the U.S. and Israel, marking a turning point where nation-states began to use cyber weapons as part of their geopolitical strategies. It emphasized how cyber capabilities could be used to achieve political objectives without traditional warfare.

- **Sony Pictures Hack:** In 2014, Sony Pictures was subjected to a severe cyberattack that resulted in the leak of unreleased films, emails, and other sensitive data. The U.S. attributed the attack to North Korea, marking it as an act of cyberwarfare. This attack showed that cyber operations could target governments and private sector entities, highlighting the necessity for both sectors to prioritize cybersecurity.

- **Petya/NotPetya:** In 2017, a ransomware attack known as NotPetya hit Ukraine's infrastructure, affecting many global firms as well. The U.S. and the UK attributed the attack to the Russian military. NotPetya served as an example of how cyberattacks could cause significant economic damage and disruption, contributing to strained relations between nation-states.

- **SolarWinds Hack:** The SolarWinds hack discovered in late 2020 was a sophisticated cyber espionage campaign that infiltrated numerous U.S. government agencies and corporations. This attack was attributed to Russia, which Russia denied. The scope and duration of the attack (it went undetected for months) underscored how cyberattacks are a persistent threat that can quietly infiltrate sensitive government and corporate systems, leading to long-term damage and challenges in attribution.

- **Exchange Server Attacks:** In early 2021, several vulnerabilities in Microsoft's Exchange Server software were exploited, allowing attackers to access thousands of networks worldwide. The U.S. attributed these attacks to a group backed by the Chinese government. This situation emphasized the global reach of cyberattacks and how they can exploit commonly used software to compromise systems.

These examples underscore the critical interplay between geopolitics and cybersecurity. They show that nation-states increasingly use cyberattacks to exert power, influence, or respond to perceived threats. Understanding the geopolitical landscape is essential to predict potential threats and develop effective cybersecurity strategies.

The Current State of International Law

Over this and the next couple of chapters, we will discuss the legal frameworks of the global community and international conventions that your organization needs to adhere to when trading either in your own country or internationally. Current laws and global agreements are struggling to keep up with the rapid advances in technology. There is nothing new in that claim, but we need to be mindful that as fast as we build and deploy new technologies, so too do the hackers and "bad actors" trying to disrupt our organizations or gain from stealing sensitive data.

There is an old saying, "Nature abhors a vacuum." In that context, where governments and global organizations have yet to provide legal frameworks to protect against cyber threats, some non-government groups, like Microsoft and the Tallinn Manual project, have started creating their own guidelines for good behavior in cyberspace. These aren't legally binding, but they're a start.

This situation presents a chance for countries to step up and make official laws, similar to what was done in the past for areas like Antarctica[5] and nuclear safety. If countries want to stay in control of the digital space and protect their interests, they must be more proactive in setting and enforcing these laws.

The global laws that govern cybersecurity are in a crisis, indicated by three primary issues:

1. Attempts to establish comprehensive, multilateral, binding cybersecurity treaties have been unsuccessful. Early efforts by France and joint efforts by Russia and China to introduce such agreements were not well received by other countries. The chances of seeing an all-encompassing treaty on this issue in the near future seem unlikely.

---

[5] The Antarctic Treaty was signed in 1959 by 12 nations and came into effect in the mid-1960s. The central ideas with full acceptance were the freedom of scientific research in Antarctica and the peaceful use of the continent. There was also a consensus for demilitarization.

2. There's a clear hesitancy from states to contribute to developing specific international customary rules around cybersecurity. Despite cyber activities playing an increasingly crucial role, nations often hold back clear expressions of their legal positions on cyber matters. This hesitation only adds to the ambiguity concerning how international law applies to cyberspace.

3. States are more likely to resort to 'norms' or guidelines instead of establishing firm rules or laws. An example is the UN's Group of Government Experts' recent report, which advocated for voluntary and non-binding norms for responsible state behavior. However, even these norms have received limited support from nations.

Given the reluctance of nation-states to establish international cybersecurity laws, it is critically important that we, as leaders, gain an understanding of the current global environment, at least for the geographies in which we do business. And this includes the laws which govern our suppliers and customers and which, as a consequence of their location, may impact us.

Having at least a basic understanding will help us to have meaningful discussions. We need to understand the international legal landscape to chart our course forward and move our business practices in the right direction, even without formal cybersecurity pacts in place.

The lack of a dedicated international legal system or set of laws for cyber activities doesn't mean that such activities are exempt from rules. As has been accepted by states, the general rules of international law apply to cyberspace conduct, too. Existing international law applies to new technology without the need to establish a completely new regulatory framework for each advance in digital technology or each new threat that emerges.

For example, the UN Charter existed when nuclear weapons were still a secret, so it doesn't explicitly mention cybersecurity in its provisions about the use of force. But, the International Court of Justice later determined that these provisions apply to any use of force, no matter the type of weapon, even if they weren't known or invented when the Charter was adopted. Alongside these general rules, certain treaties provide a 'patchwork of regulations' for cyber activities. However, these only govern a small portion of cyber-related activities or have limited membership.

So, while cyberspace isn't a lawless territory, there isn't yet a comprehensive system governing global cyber activities. States seem hesitant to develop and interpret international law for cybersecurity. This hesitation has created a power vacuum, which non-state actors have started filling with their own 'norms.'

In this critical moment for international cybersecurity law, there's no need to panic (well, not just yet, anyway). History shows that a mix of initial soft-law approaches, combined with growing binding rules, can provide a suitable framework for dealing with new technology and the emerging threats that these new technologies enable (such as deep fakes and AI). The diversity of norm-making processes involving various state and non-state actors is common in the 21st century and not inherently threatening.

It is crucial now whether and how much states will reclaim their central legislative role. Their actions in the upcoming years will decide whether we see a gradual decline in inter-state governance of cyberspace or a fundamental recalibration of legal approaches, with states again taking center stage. If states want to ensure their ability to achieve strategic and political goals isn't undermined, further hesitation may deteriorate their chances of success.

The Information Security Forum

The Information Security Forum (ISF) is a prominent group of companies from all around the world that have come together to develop practical strategies for dealing with cybersecurity issues. These organizations invest resources and share their knowledge and experiences to create methods and solutions that help businesses manage their cybersecurity risks.

One of the most significant outputs of the ISF is a document known as the Standard of Good Practice for Information Security (SGP). This is essentially a guide to identifying and managing cybersecurity risks for businesses and their supply chains. It is regularly updated, with the current version being from 2020.

Developing the SGP is a complex process that relies on four main activities:

- An extensive research and work program led by a dedicated ISF team that studies current trends and hot topics in cybersecurity. The team creates reports and develops tools that help in the management of cybersecurity.

- Analysis and incorporation of existing cybersecurity standards and legal requirements from around the world. This ensures that the SGP stays relevant and up-to-date with the latest regulations and best practices in the field.

- Input from ISF members gathered through workshops, meetings, and interviews. This helps ensure that the SGP is practical and effective, as it is based on real-world experiences of businesses dealing with cybersecurity.

- Insights from the ISF Benchmark, a tool that helps understand how cybersecurity is implemented in different member organizations.

Rather than getting bogged down in detail here, I have provided a short management guide to the ISF Standard of Good Practice in the appendices at the end of this book. The SGP is divided into 17 categories, which can be thought of as falling under three main areas:

- **Planning for Cybersecurity:** This involves developing a strategy for managing cybersecurity, identifying your IT system's specific requirements, and creating rules and procedures to manage security.

- **Managing the Cybersecurity Function:** This involves implementing and managing security measures that meet the previously identified requirements.

- **Security Assessment:** This ensures that the security measures allow business operations to continue smoothly. This also includes monitoring and continually improving the security measures in place.

In simpler terms, the SGP helps businesses figure out what they need in terms of cybersecurity, helps them put these measures in place, and ensures these measures are working effectively. The ISF and its SGP are like trusted advisors, guiding businesses through the complex world of cybersecurity.

Intellectual Property and the Value of Data

The shift from tangible to intangible assets, particularly intellectual property (IP) in the form of designs, patents, customer lists and preferences, and many other forms that IP takes and creates value for your organization. This creates new challenges in the cybersecurity landscape. Here are some of the key issues:

- **Value of IP:** Intellectual property is often at the core of a company's value proposition. From

technology firms' patents to trade secrets. Who
can forget The Colonel's famous "eleven secret
herbs and spices." Or Amazon's patented "one-
touch order." It is these unique elements that make
an organization competitive in the marketplace.
Today, most of this intellectual property is stored
digitally, making it susceptible to cyber theft. The
loss of IP can damage a company's competitive
position, decrease its market value, and erode
customer trust.

- **Increasing Attacks:** Cyberattacks targeting
  Intellectual Property (IP) have increased in both
  sophistication and number. Threat actors range
  from individual hackers to organized crime
  syndicates and even state-sponsored groups.
  Techniques such as spear-phishing, ransomware,
  and Advanced Persistent Threats (APTs) are
  commonly used to gain unauthorized access to
  sensitive information. Once inside a network, these
  threat actors can spend months exploring and
  extracting valuable IP data in poorly protected
  digital spaces.

- **International Tensions:** Intellectual property theft,
  particularly when it involves state actors, can
  create significant international tensions.
  Accusations of IP theft can lead to diplomatic
  fallout and economic sanctions and even
  contribute to broader conflicts. Balancing national
  security concerns with the need for international
  cooperation in cybersecurity is a delicate task.

- **Difficulties in Protection and Detection:**
  Protecting intellectual property is complex due to
  the increasing sophistication of attacks and the
  expanding digital landscape. Many organizations
  now use a mix of on-premises, cloud, and hybrid
  infrastructure, along with an array of devices that
  can access sensitive data. Ensuring consistent
  security measures across all these areas is a
  challenge. Furthermore, the stealthy nature of
  modern cyberattacks means that breaches can go
  undetected for a long time, giving attackers ample
  opportunity to steal intellectual property. In many
  cases, the hacker will onsell their knowledge of
  your weaknesses to others, intent on doing harm
  or gaining an advantage.

- **Legal and Regulatory Compliance:** Regulations
  around data protection and privacy, such as the
  GDPR in the European Union or the CCPA in
  California, require businesses to secure the
  personal data they hold. While these laws don't
  specifically target IP, a breach that reveals a failure
  to protect sensitive data could have legal
  implications and lead to substantial fines, not to
  mention reputational damage.

- **Third-Party Risks:** As companies increasingly
  outsource and form partnerships, they often need
  to share their IP with third parties. These partners
  may not have the same level of cybersecurity
  defenses as the IP owner, making them attractive
  targets for cybercriminals. A breach of a third
  party can lead to the exposure or theft of the

company's IP. How does this apply? If you have provided designs or manufacturing specifications to your suppliers so that they can produce component parts for your finished product, does that third-party supplier have appropriate cybersecurity defenses to protect your IP assets? Is their supply change and logistics systems tied into yours, such that a breach of their systems would provide a malicious actor with access to your systems?

- **Insider Threats:** It's not only external threats that organizations need to worry about—insider threats are also a serious concern. Disgruntled or malicious employees, or those simply unaware of security best practices, can inadvertently or deliberately cause a breach, leading to IP theft.

These challenges highlight the importance of robust cybersecurity measures to protect intellectual property. Businesses need to conduct regular risk assessments, invest in advanced security technologies, and foster a culture of cybersecurity awareness throughout the organization. Additionally, building strong relationships with law enforcement and participating in information-sharing initiatives can help companies stay ahead of emerging threats.

Case Study: McAfee's Response

As described by Allison Cerra,[6] McAfee's new website was hacked on Easter Sunday in 2017, *"Someone had deliberately defaced the social profile of our newly minted, 12-day-old company social media platform with the most obscene and offensive language directed at nearly every walk of life."*

McAfee, a computer security company, experienced a very intense incident of cyber intrusion on a major social media platform, impacting the company's reputation. The actions Cerra and her team undertook to rectify the situation and handle the crisis were crucial. Here are some takeaways and considerations from the story:

Always Be Prepared: The Boy Scouts motto, "Be prepared," is well known to everyone. The very first line of this book is, *"If it hasn't happened to your business already, it will!"*. The message here is that you have been warned. An attack is no longer an unforeseen event. It is going to happen. **Be Prepared!** As a leader in your organization, you want your business to be ready to respond swiftly to a cyberattack. Companies must have crisis management plans that include communication chains and rapid-response actions to counteract an attack that is coming. It's not enough to manage the situation— you also need to effectively communicate how you rose to the occasion and demonstrate how your plans worked. It's like that old saying, *"Democracy not only needs to be done, it needs to be seen to be done."* Not only does this build trust inside your

---

[6] Allison Cerra "The Cybersecurity Playbook" 2019.

organization and with your community of stakeholders, it sends a strong message to would be threat actors. *Cybersecurity not only needs to be done, it needs to be seen to be done!*

How you communicate internally within the company during the crisis, keeping everyone informed and alerted, is a key aspect of crisis management. Such communication not only helps manage the situation but also ensures that employees feel involved and can take any necessary actions from their end.

In the McAfee case study, the CEO's engagement and commitment to addressing the issue potentially expedited the resolution process. In other examples, we have seen positive senior executive engagement made a huge difference. The Tylenol story[7] from 1982 is another such example. These positive engagements underscore the value of networking and maintaining good relationships within the industry, which can come in handy during crises.

The decision to share the incident with the entire company the next day was a brave step and a good example of leading with transparency. By doing so, Cerra helped the employees understand the situation better and ensured everyone was aware of what had happened.

Lastly, this incident highlights the significance of robust cybersecurity measures and practices. From multi-factor authentication to monitoring suspicious activities, cybersecurity is not just about protecting servers but

---

[7] https://en.wikipedia.org/wiki/Chicago_Tylenol_murders.

protecting and monitoring all digital and physical platforms and systems a company uses.

In the future, it would be wise to conduct regular security audits, enhance training programs on cybersecurity for employees, and ensure multi-factor authentication for all critical platforms. Always remember the digital landscape is evolving, and so are the security threats. Hence, keeping up-to-date with the latest security practices and protocols is essential.

In all, despite the negative impact, such incidents can serve as a valuable lesson for companies further to strengthen their cybersecurity measures and crisis management strategies.

Information Warfare on a Global Scale

At its core, the issue of intellectual property (IP) theft can highlight a fundamental difference in cultural and philosophical values between, for example, the U.S. and China.

From the American perspective, IP (patents, trademarks, and copyrights) is the lifeblood of innovation. This belief is deeply rooted in a culture that prizes individualism, entrepreneurial spirit, and the right to profit from one's ideas. IP laws are seen as the guarantor of these rights, creating a secure environment for creativity and invention by ensuring inventors can reap the rewards of their labor. Indeed, one of the fundamental principles of Western legal frameworks and the bedrock of capitalism is the protection of private property, of which IP is a significant driver of wealth and value.

In contrast, China's cultural and political history frames IP differently. Historically, China has emphasized the collective over the individual. Knowledge and ideas are viewed as communal goods meant for the benefit of society at large rather than individual profit. This perspective doesn't lend itself naturally to the concept of IP rights as understood in the West. Hence, China's lax attitude (as seen from a Western perspective) towards IP protection has occasionally led to allegations of theft.

The divergence in cultural values gets magnified when we consider the implications on the world stage. For the U.S., losing IP means more than just lost revenue—it's about losing a competitive edge, potentially jeopardizing national security, and shifting global power dynamics. This fear is not unfounded. A United States Trade Representative report suggested that the cost of Chinese theft of American IP ranges between $225 billion and $600 billion annually.

China, on the other hand, is on a mission to elevate itself as a global tech superpower. In many areas, they are playing catch-up, and the acquisition of foreign IP, by fair means or foul, has in the past offered a fast track to technological parity.[8] On the other hand, China is leading in many areas of digital and cyber research and commercial exploitation, as measured by the number of patents issued annually. In

---

[8] In 2003, Cisco sued Huawei for IP theft.

the field of artificial intelligence, as just one example, since 2018, China has surpassed Germany, Japan, and South Korea for patents awarded, and it is almost equal to the United States.[9]

This has given birth to a new form of conflict: information warfare. This isn't just about stealing blueprints or hacking databases. It's a broad spectrum of activities, including spreading disinformation, cyber-espionage, and even direct cyberattacks on critical infrastructure. It's a silent war fought not on physical battlegrounds but in the depths of cyberspace. This is absolutely not a one-way street. All governments are engaged in information warfare to greater or lesser degrees. Keep in mind the disclosures by Edward Snowden about what the NSA gets involved in and the case study mentioned in Chapter 2 about "The Shadow Brokers" acting on apparently stolen U.S. NSA hacking tools.

The 2015 agreement between President Obama and President Xi attempted to create some 'rules of the road' for behavior in this new digital battlefield. However, defining and enforcing these rules remains challenging due to the digital world's inherent complexity and constantly evolving nature.

Ultimately, IP theft is a flashpoint in a larger geopolitical tension-filled landscape. It reflects the underlying economic disparities, power dynamics, and differing governance and global order views. To navigate this complex issue, a comprehensive approach addressing these larger conflicts is needed—forming a global consensus on

---

[9] www.iamip.com.

digital conduct, enhancing cybersecurity measures, and fostering mutual respect for cultural differences.

In discussing intellectual property (IP) theft, it's important to recognize the complexities within the issue. Here are a few more dimensions to consider:

- **The Evolving Nature of IP Theft:** In today's digital age, IP theft has evolved beyond the simple act of stealing a physical blueprint. It now encompasses cyber espionage, digital theft, software reverse engineering, and unauthorized technology replication. For example, a company's trade secrets can be stolen via a simple email phishing scam or by infiltrating complex databases. This evolution makes IP theft more difficult to prevent, detect, and prosecute.

- **The Role of State-Backed Entities:** IP theft is not solely the work of independent hackers or businesses. In numerous cases, government-backed entities have been implicated. These can be state-owned companies that directly benefit from stolen IP or cyber units within the government or military that carry out hacking operations. I am cautious in using the term, "foreign-state-backed entities." I am Australian, so foreign for me is different to a person in the U.S., China, or even New Zealand. You need to be aware that almost every government and military organization on the planet has the capability, if not the intent, to engage in state-backed cyber hacking.

- **Technological Dependencies and Supply Chains:**
Most companies are intertwined with international
suppliers and businesses in their supply chains. In
times gone past, these international relations were
the preserve of large multinationals. Not so
anymore. Home-based businesses providing
Internet-based e-commerce are involved in global
trade. Your Apple iPhone is the product of
between ten and fifteen countries, contributing to
the global supply chain, resourcing, and
manufacturing of the device you hold in your hand.
These complex relationships often lead to
technology transfer—sometimes voluntary,
sometimes not—which can be a pathway to IP
theft. Moreover, some companies, eager to tap into
vast international markets, have been known to
share their technology willingly, a practice that has
raised controversy and regulatory scrutiny.

- **Legal and Regulatory Challenges:** Even though
the World Trade Organization (WTO) and
international IP treaties provide some framework
for dealing with IP theft, enforcement remains a
significant challenge. Countries have different legal
systems and standards of evidence. Actions that
are illegal in one country may not be seen as illegal
in another. This makes it difficult to prosecute
offenses, particularly across international borders.

- **Economic Implications:** While it's clear that IP
theft has economic impacts, the scale is difficult to
quantify. The figures often cited are estimates at
best. However, it's not just about direct financial

loss. IP theft can also discourage innovation if companies fear their ideas will be stolen, and this can have long-term economic consequences.

- **Diplomatic Ramifications:** The issue of IP theft has been a source of tension between the U.S. and China,[10] straining relations and contributing to the broader trade war between the two countries. It's a complex problem that demands diplomatic finesse and negotiation. However, given the strategic and economic stakes, it's not an issue that can be easily swept under the rug.

The situation highlights the need for strengthened global cyber norms and improved cross-border law enforcement cooperation. It also underscores the importance of strong cybersecurity measures within businesses. While geopolitical and legal solutions are pursued, companies must aggressively protect their IP, using the latest in encryption, threat detection, and incident response technologies.

---

[10] U.S. House of Representatives resolution—"select committee on the strategic competition between the United States and the Chinese communist party" was passed on January 10th 2023.

What Did You Do in the War, Grandpa?

To tackle the issue of cybersecurity and intellectual property theft, we need to lay out a comprehensive overview of the shift in warfare and conflict from traditional to digital and asymmetrical. Let's take a moment to delve further into the role of private entities in this new paradigm:

The Private Sector's Role in Digital Warfare

Companies are now on the front lines of digital warfare. Not only are they often the victims of cyberattacks aiming to steal their intellectual property or disrupt their operations, but they also play a crucial part in securing digital spaces.

Many of the most innovative developments in cybersecurity technology are coming from the private sector, which can be more agile and creative than state-run entities. These businesses can often detect and react to threats more quickly, and their cooperation and collaboration can be vital in defending against or mitigating cyberattacks.

Beyond their own operations, private companies like banks, telecoms, retailers, and other suppliers form the backbone of information sharing, enabling business activities across sectors. As cyber threats often target these entities first to access broader networks, private companies are well-positioned as the first line of detection and defense against attacks propagating through their systems and assets. Their infrastructure serves as conduits for business transactions and traffic flows, presenting vulnerabilities that malicious actors seek to exploit. By securing their own assets against intrusions, private companies can strengthen cyber protections for the interconnected networks relied upon by the whole business ecosystem.

The key focus is on how private companies form a core business network that sees and can defend against threats before they spread more widely.

Legal Framework and Private Entities

While the private sector is becoming increasingly active in defense against cyber threats, its actions must be bound by a legal framework that respects both domestic and international law.

In the global digital landscape, a cyberattack against a company can quickly evolve into an international incident. Therefore, private entities must be cautious in responding to these threats. A "hack-back" might be perceived as a hostile act by a foreign government, potentially leading to escalating tensions or even conflict.

At the same time, companies have a right and a responsibility to protect their assets and customers. Existing legal frameworks might not fully address the complexities of digital warfare, particularly regarding the rights and responsibilities of private entities. Hence, new laws and regulations might be required to address these challenges.

Common Ground Across Jurisdictions

It's important to find common ground among different national legal systems to combat digital threats and protect intellectual property. Cyber threats are a global problem and solving them requires global cooperation.

The development of international norms and agreements, as well as the strengthening of multinational organizations that deal with cyber issues, can help provide a unified front against cyber threats. Cooperation, information sharing, and mutual assistance can strengthen everyone's defense and lead to better overall cybersecurity.

In conclusion, navigating the current era of digital warfare requires a careful balancing act between aggressive defense and diplomatic cooperation, both at the state level and in the private sector. Companies, governments, and international organizations must work together, respecting the rule of law, to protect against cyber threats and maintain the stability of the global order.

In a Nutshell

The economic value of Intellectual Property (IP) and data has skyrocketed in the context of our digital era, driven by the advancement of technology and the shift towards information-based economies. This trend is even more pronounced due to the influence of geopolitical powers, or hegemonies, that hold significant sway in the global arena. As data becomes the new oil, cyberattack incentives have correspondingly escalated.

The relationship between IP, data monetization, and cyber threats is intricately tied to the undercurrents of geopolitical power. Countries with advanced technological capabilities often have the most valuable IP and data assets. This makes them prime targets for cyberattacks from state and non-state actors alike.

On the other hand, geopolitical dynamics also dictate the measures taken to safeguard these valuable assets. Cybersecurity technologies, such as firewalls, antivirus software, encryption tools, and AI-based threat detection systems, play a crucial role in this defense strategy.

The service provision aspect of cybersecurity is another crucial dimension. It's not just about the technology used to protect data and IP but also about the strategies, policies, and human resources deployed. Providing *cybersecurity services* is another key part of the overall cybersecurity program. It's not only about the technology used to protect data and IP. It's also about the plans, policies, and people involved. For example, cybersecurity leaders need to:

- Give employees regular cybersecurity training

- Have strict rules about who can access systems and data

- Make sure systems get regular updates and backups

- Have plans ready for responding to cyberattacks

This involves more than just having the right tools. Leaders must also use good strategies, policies, and staff training to provide full cybersecurity services.

As cybersecurity leaders navigate this complex landscape, they need a comprehensive understanding of the factors driving cyber threats. Understanding the means (how cyberattacks are carried out), motives (why they are carried out), and opportunities (when and where they are likely to occur) is critical in developing an effective cybersecurity strategy.

This chapter has given a high-level overview of these issues. While it's not exhaustive, it provides a solid foundation for cybersecurity leaders to understand the landscape and make informed decisions about their cybersecurity strategies and technologies. Leaders must stay abreast of the latest cybersecurity trends, threats, and best practices.

Key Messages

- Intellectual property and data have become extremely valuable assets and core to competitive advantage in the digital economy.

- Cyberattacks aimed at stealing IP and data are increasing in scale and sophistication, often involving state-sponsored groups.

- Different cultural attitudes toward IP underlie tensions between countries like the U.S. and China over alleged IP theft.

- IP theft can have major economic, national security, and geopolitical ramifications, straining international relations.

- Protecting IP poses challenges due to supply chain complexity, legal/regulatory gaps, third-party risks, and insider threats.

- Information warfare via cyber espionage, attacks, and disinformation campaigns is a new digital battlefield between state and non-state actors.

- Private sector plays a crucial role in cybersecurity defense but faces constraints compared to state adversaries.

- Finding common ground in international law and norms is key, but enforcement remains difficult across borders.

- Comprehensive cybersecurity strategies need to balance defense, diplomacy, and international cooperation in the face of IP theft threats.

Four

Cybersecurity Law

C ybersecurity threats are not just "bad actors" but can also include "bad laws" in foreign countries. And when I say 'foreign country,' this means any country other than your home country (which passport you carry) or the home country of your business or organization.

This book provides you with the knowledge of what is happening in the cybersecurity world. I have avoided, as far as possible, straying into providing personal opinions or interpretations. Please read the explanations in this book and draw conclusions appropriate for you and your circumstances. However, I need to provide some editorial comments on the topics in this chapter. I need to provide you with my interpretation and what I consider an appropriate warning.

The U.S. CLOUD Act (Clarifying Lawful Overseas Use of Data)[11] presents a complex legal landscape for any organization that utilizes the technology, and in particular cloud services, of businesses headquartered in the U.S. And that means, for most of us operating businesses locally in our geographies or globally in support of our customers–the vendors which we rely upon–Microsoft, Apple, Amazon, Oracle, Google, etc., are subject to the U.S. CLOUD Act.

I will explain my concerns in the context of my home country, Australia. For Australian business and government users of American technology providers, the provisions of the U.S. CLOUD Act may conflict with Australia's data protection laws (Australian Privacy Provisions), creating challenges in how data is handled and the obligations that you as an organization have with respect to that data.

I will highlight one key concern before moving on to a more general discussion of the U.S. CLOUD Act and the European Union's GDPR–the two dominant programs.

Under Australian Law, consistent with EU GDPR standards, if a Court issues a warrant demanding that you hand over data about one of your clients, or perhaps even your own organization, you are legally required to (a) inform the target of the investigation, or (b) if you are the target then you must be informed. The U.S. CLOUD Act does not necessarily require a court order. Instead, an American law enforcement agency can pursue what is called a "warrantless search." The second, and bigger issue, is that

---

11 U.S. Legislators had to work extra hard to come up with an acronym that matched cloud computing.

under the U.S. CLOUD Act, it is an offence for the technology provider to inform the target of an investigation that their data has been retrieved. This means that if you host your data on the cloud service of a U.S. business, anywhere in the world, U.S. law enforcement is legally entitled to demand your data, and your technology provider is legally required to keep that request a secret from you.

The U.S. Approach to Cybersecurity Law

The U.S. CLOUD Act was enacted in 2018. The Act establishes procedures for U.S. law enforcement to access data located in other countries, addressing gaps (as perceived by U.S. regulators) in the scope of law enforcement tools and privacy laws. This Act also establishes procedures for foreign governments to make direct law enforcement requests to U.S. service providers, streamlining compliance. Moreover, the Act formalizes processes for companies to challenge law enforcement requests and imposes limits to address privacy and civil liberty concerns.

The CLOUD Act is a game changer in the field of cyber law and data storage.[12] This legislation allows U.S. law enforcement to access data stored overseas under certain

---

12 As stated at the beginning of this chapter. The U.S. CLOUD Act applies globally to every U.S. Company.

conditions. This is crucial in the era of cloud computing, where data is often stored across multiple jurisdictions. Here's a simplified look at what it means for businesses:

- **Access to Overseas Data:** In essence, the CLOUD Act means that if your business uses electronic communication or cloud computing services, like email or file storage provided by, or use the products supplied by U.S.-based technology companies and service providers, then U.S. law enforcement can potentially access your data regardless of where it's physically stored.

- **Foreign Governments Requests:** The CLOUD Act also establishes a framework for foreign governments to request access to data held in the U.S. or by U.S. companies. They can do so directly rather than through a complex treaty process, which can speed up law enforcement and investigative processes. However, to make such requests, the foreign government must have an agreement with the U.S. and meet specific privacy and civil liberties protection criteria.

- **Legal Challenges:** If your company is asked to hand over data and you believe that doing so would violate the laws of your home country or pose a significant risk to your organization, then you have the right to challenge this request—if you are made aware of the request. In here lies the Catch-22 of the CLOUD Act. The CLOUD Act provides a formal process for you to raise a legal concern, which includes notifying the foreign (to the U.S.) government concerned. The problem

(Catch-22) is that the CLOUD Act makes it illegal for the U.S. service provider to inform you of the request to access your data.

- **Executive Agreements:** The CLOUD Act introduces the concept of 'Executive Agreements' between the U.S. and other countries. These agreements essentially streamline the process for data access and provide clarity to companies who were previously stuck between conflicting laws of different countries. Once an agreement is in place, your company can comply with a request from a foreign government without fear of violating U.S. laws.

- **Privacy Considerations:** The CLOUD Act also considers privacy and civil liberty concerns. For instance, it doesn't require companies to create 'backdoors' for decryption. It also sets limitations on the types of requests from foreign law enforcement under these agreements, such as requiring specific identification of people, accounts, or devices, and limitations on time and scope.

- **Implications for Business Decisions:** With the implementation of the CLOUD Act, your business needs to carefully consider where your data is stored. This is particularly relevant if the country where the data is stored has an Executive Agreement with the U.S. This could influence the choices your business makes about data storage and management and could help avoid legal complications.

In essence, the CLOUD Act is intended to simplify and clarify the process for U.S. Law Enforcement Agencies to access data across borders. As a business leader, it's important to understand these changes and to adapt your data storage and management strategies accordingly. In the European Union, a lot of organizations are strengthening their data management by ensuring that all data is stored in an encrypted form.

As a leader in business or government, you need to be aware of the potential downside risks for organizations outside the United States. You need to pay particular attention to a range of issues that could have very serious consequences for the information that your systems store and manage:

- **Jurisdiction Conflicts:** If your company is based in a country with strict privacy laws, complying with a U.S. request for data under the CLOUD Act might put you in conflict with your local laws. This could lead to legal challenges, fines, and damage to your reputation within your home jurisdiction.

- **Customer Trust Issues:** The knowledge that data might be accessed by U.S. law enforcement could deter customers who are concerned about privacy. This is particularly true for customers in regions with strong data protection regulations or where there's a general distrust of foreign government intervention. Europeans, for example, are very wary of government overreach, and there is significant concern about organizations in Europe complying with demands from U.S. regulators.

Many European service providers make it clear that all data is encrypted for this reason.

- **Increased Complexity:** Understanding and complying with the CLOUD Act might require substantial legal expertise, especially if there's an Executive Agreement between the U.S. and the country where your business operates. This can add complexity and cost to your operations.

- **Potential for Overreach:** Concerns have been raised that the CLOUD Act might be used in ways that go beyond its stated intent. For example, a broad interpretation of the law might allow for data requests that are more sweeping than necessary for a given investigation, potentially putting unnecessary data at risk.

- **Risk of Inconsistent Interpretation:** Without clear, universal standards for inter-agency cooperation, there may be inconsistencies in how the CLOUD Act is interpreted and applied in different countries. This can create business uncertainty, particularly in countries without Executive Agreements with the United States. Australian authorities, for example, regularly exercise exemption clauses in our privacy principles to satisfy a request from U.S. authorities seeking data from systems operating in Australia. By contrast, the European Commission has proposed a new law (July 2023) to enhance collaboration between data protection authorities (DPAs) in cross-border cases under the General Data Protection Regulation by introducing procedural rules and early sharing of key investigation details to foster consensus and reduce disagreements from the outset.

- **Potential Impact on Service Providers:** The CLOUD Act might impact your competitive positioning if you're a cloud or communication service provider. Customers concerned with privacy might prefer providers that are less likely to be subject to U.S. jurisdiction, which could sway businesses away from your services.

- **Challenges to Local Sovereignty:** For governments outside the U.S., the CLOUD Act may be seen as a challenge to local sovereignty. Even though the Act includes provisions for objections and legal challenges, the potential for U.S. law enforcement to access data without going through local legal processes can be contentious.

- **Risk to Intellectual Property:** The potential access to sensitive information could pose a threat to intellectual property and trade secrets for companies. If this information were to be disclosed inappropriately, it could lead to competitive disadvantages.

In summary, the CLOUD Act represents a significant change in the way data can be accessed across borders, and it introduces a range of new considerations for businesses outside the U.S. Careful evaluation of these factors, possibly in consultation with legal experts, will be necessary for businesses to navigate these new challenges effectively.

States versus Federal Laws

The United States and the European Union (EU) approach the regulation of artificial intelligence (AI) and data privacy from fundamentally different governance frameworks, leading to distinct challenges and operational dynamics. In the U.S., the principle of "States' Rights" embedded in the federal system complicates the creation of unified federal legislation on AI and data privacy. In contrast, the EU benefits from a more 'harmonized' approach due to its supranational legal structure.

In the United States, the federal system of government allows states considerable autonomy to enact their laws and regulations, including those governing technology, AI, and data privacy. This system stems from the Tenth Amendment of the U.S. Constitution, which reserves all powers not explicitly granted to the federal government to the states or the people. As a result:

- **Diverse Regulatory Approaches**: Each state can develop rules and standards that reflect local values, economic interests, and political priorities. For instance, California has implemented comprehensive privacy laws like the California Consumer Privacy Act (CCPA), while other states may have less stringent regulations. This creates a mosaic of regulatory environments across the country.

- **Complex Compliance Landscape**: This diversity requires navigating a complex patchwork of state laws for businesses operating nationwide. Companies must ensure compliance with the varying requirements of each state in which they operate, which can be resource-intensive and lead to inefficiencies.

- **Challenges in Establishing Federal Legislation**: The principle of States' Rights can also lead to significant hurdles in passing unified federal legislation. State governments and their representatives in Congress may resist federal laws that pre-empt state authority, particularly if those federal laws are perceived as less favorable than existing state regulations. This can lead to significant delays, amendments, or the watering down of federal initiatives to gain broad acceptance.

EU's Harmonized Regulatory Framework

Contrastingly, the EU operates under a different system where directives and regulations are designed to harmonize laws across member states:

- **Unified Legal Framework:** The EU can enact laws such as the General Data Protection Regulation (GDPR), which member states are obligated to implement. This ensures a consistent approach to AI and data privacy across all member countries.

- **Simpler Compliance for Businesses:** The harmonized rules reduce the regulatory burden for businesses operating across the EU. A company compliant in one member state is generally compliant throughout the union, fostering a more integrated market and reducing operational complexities.

- **Stronger Negotiating Position:** The EU's unified approach also gives it a stronger stance in international negotiations and standards setting, allowing it to push for its regulatory frameworks as global standards.

Divergent Approaches

The principle of States' Rights in the U.S. creates a challenging environment for the development of federal AI and data privacy legislation, reflecting broader issues of federalism in the country. In comparison, the EU's more centralized approach under its harmonized rules offers clarity and consistency but may sacrifice some degree of local tailoring and flexibility that state-specific regulations in the U.S. can provide. Each system has its strengths and weaknesses, influencing how effectively each can navigate the complexities of modern technological governance.

California

California has long been at the forefront of technology regulation in the U.S., and its approach to AI legislation is no exception. The California Consumer Privacy Act (CCPA) is the most prominent example, setting a benchmark for privacy rights that has influenced discussions about federal privacy legislation. Enacted in 2018 and subsequently amended, the CCPA provides robust consumer rights regarding access to, deleting, and controlling personal information. It requires businesses to disclose their data collection and sharing practices and gives consumers the right to opt-out of the sale of their personal information.

Moreover, the CCPA includes provisions that directly address AI through transparency measures. These require businesses to disclose the logic involved in decision-making processes, thus ensuring that AI systems are not black boxes to the consumers they affect. This focus on transparency is intended to foster greater consumer trust and accountability in automated systems that make significant decisions impacting individuals' lives, such as credit scoring and personalized advertising.

Washington State

Washington State's approach to AI regulation underscores a specific concern with privacy and civil liberties, particularly regarding surveillance technologies. In 2020, Washington passed Senate Bill 6280, which specifically regulates the use of facial recognition technologies by state and local government agencies. This law is significant because it addresses the ethical implications and potential abuses of facial recognition, a prevalent AI application.

Under the law, government agencies in Washington must test their facial recognition services to ensure they do not produce unfair performance differences across different demographic groups. The law also mandates public disclosure of such technologies, including accountability measures requiring agencies to produce transparency reports and implement oversight mechanisms. This legislative action reflects growing concerns about privacy, consent, and the potential for racial bias in automated facial recognition systems.

Illinois

Illinois has targeted AI transparency within the employment sector through the Artificial Intelligence Video Interview Act, which came into effect in 2020. This legislation addresses the increasing use of AI in hiring processes, particularly the deployment of AI-driven video interview platforms that analyze applicants' responses. The law mandates that employers disclose the use of AI in video interviews and provide information on how the technology works and what general types of characteristics it evaluates.

Furthermore, Illinois requires employers to obtain consent from applicants before using these AI systems, thereby empowering candidates to opt out of potentially biased automated evaluations. The act also stipulates that employers must delete any video or copies of interviews within a month of the applicant's request unless the applicant provides permission for their longer retention. This law underscores the critical importance of transparency and informed consent in using AI technologies that can significantly impact employment opportunities.

Colorado

Colorado is making significant strides in regulating artificial intelligence (AI), reflecting a broader national and global trend toward establishing legal frameworks to govern the ethical use of AI technologies. The state's proactive approach is exemplified by legislation such as Senate Bill 205, which addresses key areas of concern, including discrimination, transparency, and accountability in AI applications. This legislation highlights Colorado's commitment to ensuring that AI systems are used in a way that protects citizens and promotes fairness.

One of the central aims of Senate Bill 205 is to safeguard consumers from AI systems that might discriminate based on various personal attributes. This is particularly pertinent in contexts where AI decision-making could affect individual rights and opportunities, such as employment, housing, healthcare, and access to services. The bill requires that AI systems used in such sensitive decision-making processes are designed and operated in a manner that prevents discriminatory outcomes. This involves setting legal standards for fairness and requiring regular audits and reporting to ensure compliance.

The focus on discrimination is driven by increasing awareness of the biases embedded in AI algorithms, whether through the data used to train them or the algorithms' design. By mandating safeguards against such biases, Colorado aims to foster an environment where technology enhances societal equity rather than undermining it.

Another pivotal aspect of Colorado's legislative approach under Senate Bill 205 is requiring AI developers to be transparent about their systems' functionalities and potential risks. AI developers must disclose how their systems operate, the decisions they can make, and the data they utilize. This transparency is crucial for several reasons:

- **Informed Consent:** Ensuring that users and consumers of AI technologies are fully informed about how their data is being used and for what purposes.

- **Accountability:** Understanding how AI systems function makes it easier to hold developers and deployers accountable for any issues or adverse outcomes that may arise.

- **Risk Mitigation:** Disclosure of potential risks helps pre-emptively identify and mitigate possible harms emerging from AI systems, safeguarding public welfare.

Such disclosures empower consumers and regulatory bodies and foster trust in AI technologies, which are essential for their sustainable integration into everyday life.

The Colorado AI Insurance Regulations represent a significant legislative step in tailoring the management of artificial intelligence applications, specifically within the insurance sector. Recognizing the unique challenges and risks associated with deploying AI technologies in insurance, Colorado has introduced regulations to ensure that insurers not only embrace the benefits of AI but also mitigate potential risks effectively. These regulations are structured around two key pillars: Risk Management and Data Protection Assessments, which are designed to foster a responsible, secure, and ethical approach to the use of AI in the insurance industry.

Under the new regulations, insurance companies operating in Colorado are required to establish comprehensive AI governance and risk management frameworks. These frameworks are not merely guidelines but mandatory measures that insurers must integrate into their daily operations. The aim is to ensure that all AI systems used by insurers are overseen with high scrutiny and governed by clear policies that address potential risks throughout the AI lifecycle—from development and deployment to the continuous monitoring of AI systems:

- **Transparency:** Insurers must be transparent about how AI systems make decisions, particularly those that impact policyholders. This includes explaining the basis on which AI makes underwriting decisions or how it processes claims.

- **Accountability:** Insurance institutions must have clear lines of accountability to oversee AI systems. This ensures that a human element always manages and evaluates AI outputs.

- **Ethical Considerations:** The frameworks must consider ethical implications, ensuring that AI systems operate without bias, respect privacy, and do not result in discriminatory outcomes.

This proactive approach aims to integrate AI into the insurance sector safely and responsibly, ensuring that technology serves the best interests of both the insurers and the insured.

Another cornerstone of the Colorado AI Insurance Regulations is the requirement for regular data protection assessments. These assessments are crucial for processes involving sensitive data, which can include everything from personal health information to financial data in the context of insurance.

Maryland

Maryland has taken a significant step towards strengthening data privacy and consumer protection with the recent enactment of the Maryland Online Data Privacy Act of 2024 (MODPA). This legislation is a clear response to growing concerns about the pervasive reach of digital technologies into personal lives and the potential misuse of personal information in the digital age. MODPA introduces comprehensive measures aimed at putting control back into the hands of consumers and imposing stringent obligations on businesses handling personal data.

At the heart of MODPA is the principle of data minimization, which compels companies to rethink how they collect and store personal information. The act mandates that businesses limit their collection of personal data to what is strictly necessary for delivering their services. This approach seeks to curb the excessive and often unnecessary data collection practices that have become commonplace in the digital economy, reducing the risk of exploiting personal data for unapproved purposes. By enforcing data minimization, Maryland aims to ensure that the privacy of its residents is respected and that companies are more deliberate and transparent about the data they collect.

MODPA sets even higher standards for handling sensitive data, which includes information about racial or ethnic origin, political opinions, religious beliefs, biometric data, health, sexual orientation, and more. The act prohibits the collection, processing, or sharing of sensitive data unless it is essential for the specific services requested by a consumer. This stringent requirement compels businesses to carefully assess their data practices and implement robust safeguards to protect sensitive information, thereby enhancing trust and security for consumers who may feel vulnerable about sharing their details.

Another cornerstone of MODPA is the broad rights granted to consumers regarding their data. These rights significantly empower Maryland residents to take control of their personal information in several ways:

- **Right to Access:** Consumers can request to see the personal data a company has collected about them.

- **Right to Correction:** Consumers can correct inaccurate or incomplete data.

- **Right to Deletion:** Consumers can request the deletion of their data when it is no longer necessary for the purpose for which it was collected.

- **Right to Data Portability:** Consumers can obtain and reuse personal data across different services.

- **Right to Opt-Out:** Consumers can refuse the processing of their data for certain purposes, such as direct marketing, sale of data, or automated decision-making.

To comply with MODPA, businesses must establish clear policies and practices that align with the act's principles. This includes updating privacy policies, implementing procedures to respond to consumer requests, and conducting regular data protection assessments to identify risks. Moreover, businesses must ensure adequate systems to protect the data they collect, both from external breaches and internal misuse.

U.S. Federal Initiatives

The proposed U.S. AI Act represents a pivotal development in the federal government's approach to managing the burgeoning field of artificial intelligence (AI). As AI technologies become more integrated into various sectors of the economy and daily life, there is a growing need to address the potential security and safety risks associated with their deployment. The U.S. AI Act seeks to address these concerns through two primary initiatives: establishing a Voluntary AI Incident Database and strengthening the National Vulnerability Database to include AI security vulnerabilities.

Voluntary AI Incident Database

One of the cornerstone elements of the U.S. AI Act is the creation of a Voluntary AI Incident Database. This initiative fosters a collaborative environment where public and private sector entities can share information about AI security and safety incidents. By encouraging transparency and the exchange of information, the database aims to build a comprehensive resource that helps stakeholders understand and mitigate risks associated with AI systems.

The database would serve multiple purposes:

- **Knowledge Sharing:** It would act as a central repository for information on incidents involving AI systems, providing valuable insights into common vulnerabilities and emerging threats.

- **Preventive Actions:** By analyzing the data collected, researchers and developers can identify patterns or recurring issues and develop solutions or patches to prevent future occurrences.

- **Policy Development:** Regulators and policymakers could use the insights gained from the database to craft more informed, effective regulations and standards for AI safety and security.

Participation in the database would be voluntary, and mechanisms would be in place to protect the confidentiality of the information shared and the identities of those sharing it. This approach encourages maximum participation by reducing the potential legal or reputational risks of disclosing sensitive incident information.

National Vulnerability Database

The second major initiative under the U.S. AI Act is the enhancement of the National Vulnerability Database (NVD), a U.S. government repository of standards-based vulnerability management data. This database includes security checklist references, security-related software flaws, misconfigurations, product names, and impact metrics. The Act proposes expanding the NVD to specifically include AI security vulnerabilities, recognizing the unique challenges AI technologies pose.

This enhancement would involve:

- **Updating Processes and Procedures:** The NVD's processes would be updated to accommodate the unique aspects of AI vulnerabilities, which might differ significantly from traditional cybersecurity vulnerabilities due to the complexity and unpredictability of AI algorithms.

- **Special Handling for AI Vulnerabilities:** AI vulnerabilities might require different treatment, such as specialized tools or methods for detection and mitigation, which the updated NVD would aim to address.

- **Broader Scope of Vulnerabilities:** Including AI vulnerabilities in the NVD would broaden its scope, making it an even more comprehensive resource for understanding and mitigating risks across different technologies.

By integrating AI security vulnerabilities into the NVD, the Act aims to create a more robust and dynamic framework for securing AI systems against known and potential threats. This would enhance national security and promote trust in AI applications by ensuring their safety and reliability.

The Role of NIST at the Federal Level

The National Institute of Standards and Technology (NIST) plays a pivotal role in shaping the regulatory landscape for artificial intelligence (AI) technologies in the United States. While NIST does not directly regulate AI, its function in developing standards and guidelines is crucial. These standards often benchmark best practices in technology deployment, including AI, influencing public and private sector policies and strategies.

NIST's approach to AI involves a collaborative and open process with stakeholders from industry, academia, and government to ensure that the guidelines are comprehensive, practical, and forward-looking. The aim is to create a set of standards that address current technological capabilities and are adaptable to future advancements in AI technologies:

- **Transparency and Accountability**: One of the primary focuses of NIST's AI guidelines is to enhance transparency and accountability in AI systems. This is crucial in building trust among users and consumers and essential for the wider acceptance and ethical deployment of AI technologies. Standards that encourage transparency in AI algorithms help demystify AI decisions and make them more understandable to end-users.

- **Security and Privacy**: NIST also emphasizes the importance of security and privacy in AI systems. As AI increasingly handles more sensitive data, ensuring its integrity and security is paramount. NIST guidelines typically include best practices for data protection, recommendations for secure AI architectures, and protocols for continuously monitoring AI systems to detect and mitigate potential threats.

- **Fairness and Bias Mitigation**: Addressing bias in AI algorithms is another critical area for NIST. The organization develops standards that help identify, assess, and correct biases in AI systems, which is vital for ensuring that AI-driven decisions are fair and do not perpetuate existing inequalities.

Although NIST's guidelines are not legally binding, their influence on AI regulation is profound. Policymakers often consider NIST standards a trusted source of technical expertise that can inform legislation and regulatory policies. This influence is evident in various state and federal AI initiatives referencing NIST standards as compliance and risk assessment benchmarks.

Implications and Consequences

As artificial intelligence becomes increasingly integral to crucial sectors of business and society, there is a global shift towards establishing more formal oversight and improved governance of these technologies. Recognizing the growing dependency on AI, the National Institute of Standards and Technology (NIST) is leading efforts to develop comprehensive AI standards. This initiative is crucial as it ensures that AI development adheres to security, transparency, and equity principles, fostering a trustworthy technological advancement environment.

NIST's proactive role in formulating these standards is instrumental in shaping the future landscape of AI regulation in the United States. By offering detailed and forward-thinking guidelines, NIST influences legislative measures and promotes consistency in AI practices across various states and sectors. This ensures that AI technologies are implemented in a manner that is both responsible and ethical.

In parallel, state legislatures in California, Washington, and Illinois are taking significant steps to integrate AI responsibly into societal frameworks. These states have enacted laws to safeguard individual rights and establish a clear accountability framework for organizations deploying AI technologies. The regulations focus on ethical usage and transparency, setting a standard that could guide future federal rules and serve as a benchmark for other states.

Colorado's legislative approach to AI in the insurance sector further exemplifies state-level innovation in AI governance. The Colorado AI Insurance Regulations mandate provides comprehensive risk management strategies and regular data protection assessments, creating a model that other states might follow. These measures aim to protect consumers and provide guidance on using AI to enhance service quality and operational efficiency while addressing associated risks.

The Maryland Online Data Privacy Act of 2024 is another exemplary state initiative that addresses data privacy challenges directly linked to AI and digital technologies. By implementing stringent standards for data minimization and enhancing protections for sensitive data, Maryland is at the forefront of ensuring consumer privacy in the digital age.

The U.S. AI Act illustrates a significant step towards creating a robust framework for managing AI-related security and safety risks. Establishing a Voluntary AI Incident Database and enhancing the National Vulnerability Database to include AI vulnerabilities are key components of this act. These initiatives aim to build a secure digital infrastructure that supports innovation and ensures the safe deployment of AI technologies.

These state and national efforts underscore a comprehensive movement towards regulating AI more stringently. As AI technologies continue to evolve and expand their influence across various aspects of life, the frameworks developed by these legislative actions provide valuable lessons and models that could influence broader national and international AI policies. This collective legislative activity demonstrates a commitment to harnessing the benefits of AI while effectively mitigating its risks, ensuring that AI technologies contribute positively to society.

What does this mean to you?

When it comes to AI and data privacy legislation, the U.S. cannot be approached as a single market. State initiatives require conformance and adherence to divergent standards. This means that whether you are a U.S. company operating exclusively within national borders or a foreign company intending to enter the very large and lucrative U.S. market, you need to build your AI policies and performance to the highest standard to be confident of meeting federal and state obligations.

In practice, this means maintaining a focus on the European Union's ethical frameworks and treating these as the most comprehensive set of policies and frameworks that would ensure global compliance, irrespective of the market in which you operate.

The European Approach to Cybersecurity Law

The General Data Protection Regulation (GDPR) is a regulation in EU law that applies to all member countries. It came into effect on May 25, 2018,[13] replacing previous data protection laws in the EU and standardizing regulations across the region.

The main principles of the GDPR regulations are:

- **Transparency:** Organizations must be clear about how and why they're using personal data. This includes providing accessible privacy notices to individuals.

- **Consent:** Consent must be freely given, specific, informed, and unambiguous. It requires a positive opt-in and cannot be inferred from silence or inactivity.

- **Data Minimization:** This means collecting only the data that is necessary for the intended purpose without keeping excessive information.

- **Accuracy:** Organizations are responsible for ensuring that personal data is accurate and up to date, correcting it if necessary.

---

[13] The next update on GDPR is due in 2024.

- **Storage Limitation:** This involves not keeping personal data longer than necessary for the purpose for which it was collected.

- **Integrity and Confidentiality:** Data must be handled securely, using appropriate technical and organizational measures to prevent unauthorized access, disclosure, or loss.

- **Accountability:** Organizations must take responsibility for data handling and demonstrate compliance through proper documentation and governance structures.

The GDPR (General Data Protection Regulation) emphasizes protecting individual rights concerning personal data. Here's an expansion on the key rights that individuals enjoy under GDPR:

Right to be Informed

- **What It Is:** Individuals have the right to know how their data is being used, collected, and processed.
- **What It Means:** Organizations must provide clear, transparent information about using personal data, usually through privacy notices.

Right of Access

- **What It Is:** Individuals can request access to their personal data held by an organization.
- **What It Means:** Upon request, organizations must provide a copy of the personal data and information on how it's being processed.

Right to Rectification

- **What It Is:** Individuals can ask to have inaccurate or incomplete data corrected.
- **What It Means:** Organizations must correct the individual's data if it is wrong or incomplete.

Right to Erasure (Right to be Forgotten)

- **What It Is:** Individuals can request the deletion of their data in specific circumstances.
- **What It Means:** If certain conditions are met, organizations must erase an individual's personal data.

Right to Restrict Processing

- **What It Is:** Individuals can request the restriction of processing their data.
- **What It Means:** Organizations can still store the data but cannot use it. This might apply when the individual contests the accuracy of the data, for example.

Right to Data Portability

- **What It Is:** Individuals can request their data in a machine-readable format to use with another service provider.
- **What It Means:** This right allows individuals more control over their personal data, making it easier for them to switch between service providers.

Right to Object

- **What It Is:** Individuals can object to the processing of their data in certain circumstances.
- **What It Means:** This might include objecting to direct marketing or processing based on legitimate

interests or the performance of a task in the public interest.

Rights in Relation to Automated Decision Making and Profiling

- **What It Is:** Individuals have rights concerning automated decisions, including profiling, which can significantly affect them.
- **What It Means:** Individuals can request human intervention or challenge a decision made solely on automated processing, such as a computer algorithm.

The GDPR's focus on individual rights provides people with more control and say over how their personal data is handled. Organizations must be aware of these rights and establish procedures to respond to requests from individuals exercising these rights. Non-compliance can result in significant fines and reputational damage, emphasizing the importance of robust data management and data protection practices. By respecting and facilitating these rights, organizations not only comply with the law but also build trust with individuals, potentially enhancing customer loyalty and satisfaction.

Managing GDPR compliance is a complex task requiring attention across different organizational levels. Here's a more detailed breakdown of key management responsibilities under the GDPR:

Understanding Data Handling

- **Conducting Data Audits:** Managers must identify and document the types of personal data collected, stored, and processed. This involves assessing what data is held, where it came from, how it's used, and with whom it's shared.

- **Creating a Data Map:** This involves visualizing how data flows through the organization, which can help identify potential risks or weak points in data protection.

Implementing Safeguards

- **Selecting Appropriate Security Measures:** Depending on the sensitivity and volume of data processed, you, as a leader, must demand the right technical and organizational measures be enacted, such as encryption and secure access controls.
- **Regular Security Assessments:** This includes ongoing monitoring and regular testing of security systems to ensure they remain effective against potential threats.

Training and Awareness

- **Staff Training:** Everyone in the organization must understand their GDPR responsibilities. Managers must provide regular training to ensure all staff know how to securely handle personal data.
- **Creating a Culture of Compliance:** Management should foster a culture that values privacy and data protection, encouraging employees to act responsibly.

Creating and Implementing Procedures

- **Data Subject Requests:** Managers must establish clear procedures for dealing with requests from individuals exercising their rights under the GDPR. This includes timely responses to requests for access, rectification, or deletion.

- **Data Breach Response Plan:** Creating and maintaining a response plan for data breaches is vital. It should include steps to assess, contain, and report the breach, as well as notify affected individuals if required.

Appointing a Data Protection Officer (DPO)
- **Selection and Support:** You will need a DPO (Data Protection Officer) with sufficient knowledge, support, and independence to carry out their tasks. The DPO should report directly to the level of management with the authority to act swiftly and decisively.

Documentation and Record-Keeping
- **Maintaining Compliance Records:** Management must ensure that detailed records of data processing activities are maintained. This includes documenting the purposes of processing, categories of data processed, and retention periods.
- **Regular Reviews and Audits:** Regular reviews and internal audits of data protection practices help ensure ongoing compliance and identify areas for improvement.

Working with Third Parties
- **Vendor Assessment:** If third-party vendors handle personal data, managers must ensure they comply with GDPR requirements. This involves due diligence in selecting vendors and including specific contractual terms related to data protection.

Risk Assessment and Mitigation

- **Conducting Risk Assessments:** Managers should assess the risks associated with data processing activities and implement measures to mitigate those risks.
- **Implementing Privacy by Design:** This means considering privacy at the initial design stages of new processes, products, or services and throughout the complete development process.

GDPR compliance is not a one-time event but an ongoing responsibility. Management must be actively involved in overseeing and supporting the various aspects of compliance, from understanding data handling to implementing robust safeguards, training staff, working with third parties, and maintaining appropriate documentation. Failure to meet these responsibilities can lead to significant penalties, both in terms of fines and reputational damage. Therefore, taking a proactive, well-structured approach to GDPR compliance should be a top priority for all levels of management.

Non-compliance with the European Union's GDPR has with it potential penalties, which you need to be aware of. These include:

- **Fines:** The fines can be extremely severe, with two levels of administrative fines that depend on the type of infringement. The higher level is up to 4% of annual global turnover or €20 million, and the lower level is up to 2% of annual global turnover or €10 million.

- **Reputational Damage:** Non-compliance can lead to a loss of trust and damage the organization's reputation, possibly affecting customer relationships and business growth.

The GDPR represents a fundamental shift in EU data protection and privacy rights. Compliance requires a proactive approach, involving not just legal and IT departments but engaging the entire organization. Businesses must regularly review and update their practices, focusing on a culture that respects privacy and ensures responsible data management. By doing so, they not only comply with the law but also build trust with customers and stakeholders, which can be a significant competitive advantage.

As of 2024, the General Data Protection Regulation (GDPR) continues to be a cornerstone of data protection within the European Union. Significant developments and updates are shaping its evolution, aiming to address both the successes and the challenges experienced since its implementation in 2018:

- **GDPR Procedural Regulation:** The European Commission has proposed a new GDPR Procedural Regulation to streamline and standardize cooperation between Data Protection Authorities (DPAs) across the EU. This regulation aims to enhance the efficiency of cross-border enforcement by providing a more consistent procedural framework. Notably, it does not impose additional regulatory obligations on businesses but aims to grant more rights and legal certainty during enforcement actions and investigations.

- **Comprehensive Review:** A comprehensive review of the GDPR is scheduled every four years. The second iteration of this review is due in 2024, but as of yet, we have not seen what this might look like. According to the legislation, it is intended that the regular four-yearly review will assess the regulation's application, focusing on enforcement and its impact on data protection practices across the EU. There is speculation about a potential "GDPR 2.0" to address identified deficiencies and adapt to new challenges, particularly regarding international data transfers and adequacy decisions. This is reinforced by a recent ruling by the European Data Protection Supervisor, which found[14] that the European Commission had violated several provisions of the data protection laws, specifically when it comes to the international transfer of protected data held and managed by a cloud services provider outside of the European Union.

- **International Data Transfers:** The review highlights ongoing challenges with international data transfers, especially between the EU and the United States. The EU's attempts to establish stable legal frameworks for data transfers have faced legal challenges, underscoring the need for more flexible and reliable mechanisms. Adequacy decisions, while considered the most

---

[14] https://www.edps.europa.eu/press-publications/press-news/press-releases/2024/european-commissions-use-microsoft-365-infringes-data-protection-law-eu-institutions-and-bodies_en.

straightforward solution, have proven difficult to implement consistently.

- **Increased Enforcement and Litigation:** There has been a notable increase in GDPR enforcement actions and private litigation. This trend emphasizes the need for consistent and robust enforcement mechanisms across member states. The new procedural regulation aims to address this by improving cooperation and consistency among national DPAs.

- **Resource Allocation and DPO Challenges:** Investigations by the European Data Protection Board (EDPB) revealed that many organizations still struggle with appointing and adequately resourcing Data Protection Officers (DPOs). The report recommended clearer guidance and increased awareness campaigns to ensure compliance with DPO requirements, emphasizing the need for adequate resources and independence for DPOs.

The GDPR's review process in 2024 will be pivotal in determining the future direction of data protection within the EU. While a complete overhaul is unlikely, incremental updates and clarifications are expected to enhance the regulation's effectiveness and adaptability. The EU aims to maintain its high standards of data protection while addressing practical enforcement challenges and facilitating smoother international data flows.

CLOUD Act versus EU GDPR

The CLOUD Act in the U.S. and the EU's data privacy regulations, particularly GDPR, exhibit some conflicts and tensions that can create challenges for businesses operating across these jurisdictions. This is particularly problematic when your IT organization makes generic statements about GDPR compliance without fully understanding what that entails and what obligations it places on you. If your public-facing website tells your customers that you are compliant with GDPR data protections, you must understand your obligations. Here's a look at some of the primary areas of conflict:

Jurisdictional Reach:
The **GDPR** restricts the transfer of personal data outside the European Economic Area (EEA) unless meeting these conditions:

- Adequate data protection laws exist in the destination country

- Appropriate safeguards like binding agreements or rules are present

- In public interest circumstances

- Explicit consent from individuals has been provided

- Transfer to certified organizations with approved standards

The **CLOUD Act** allows U.S. authorities to demand access to data held by American companies, regardless of where the data is stored globally. The CLOUD Act grants global reach to access data, even when stored overseas. It's akin to a powerful magnet, pulling information from the furthest corners of the globe and potentially overriding local regulations and protections.

Consent and Individual Rights:

- Under **GDPR**, individuals have significant control over their personal data, including the right to be forgotten, to object, and to access their information.

- The **CLOUD Act** doesn't necessarily recognize these rights, and U.S. law enforcement access might disregard the individual rights and protections provided by the GDPR. The CLOUD Act's preclusion of user notification impedes transparency. It potentially erodes trust by depriving users of the essential rights provided by the EU's GDPR, the Australian Privacy Principles, and the laws of countries that have endorsed GDPR as a founding principle for their own approaches to data protection.

Legal Process:

- The **GDPR** emphasizes transparency, lawfulness, and fairness in data processing, which might be undermined if U.S. authorities access data without adhering to EU standards.

- The **CLOUD Act** allows U.S. law enforcement to bypass local legal processes in some cases, which may conflict with the GDPR's requirement for a legal basis for data processing and transfer.

- **Australia's Privacy Act** (which we will discuss shortly), provides an important thread in our tapestry and finds itself entangled with the CLOUD Act. Here, we encounter a clash of principles, where warrant requirements, safeguards, and notification rules collide, causing ripples of confusion and instability.

Data Protection Principles:

- The **GDPR** requires that data processing be limited to what is necessary in relation to the purpose for which it is processed. This might conflict with broad or sweeping data requests under the **CLOUD Act.**

- Under **GDPR**, businesses must implement appropriate safeguards to protect personal data, which might be compromised by compliance with a request under the **CLOUD Act.** On the positive side, the CLOUD Act serves as a bridge-builder, fostering data-sharing agreements between like-minded nations. It is meant to open doors to collaboration, forging bonds in a sometimes fractious landscape.

Potential Conflicts with Other Agreements:

- The EU and the U.S. have specific mechanisms like the Privacy Shield (which has been invalidated) and Standard Contractual Clauses to govern data transfers. The **CLOUD Act** may operate outside these frameworks, leading to potential conflicts.

Challenges for Businesses:

• Companies caught between these conflicting legal requirements 2 and regulators.

Sovereignty Concerns:

- The EU may see the extraterritorial reach of the **CLOUD Act** as an infringement on its sovereignty and legal autonomy, particularly if U.S. authorities are seen to be bypassing or undermining European legal processes.

These conflicts highlight the complex legal landscape for international data access and privacy, especially for businesses that operate in both the U.S. and the EU. They may require careful navigation, legal consultation, and collaboration between different jurisdictions to resolve.

Management of data rights and privacy is a complex battleground where the U.S. CLOUD Act works to enable law enforcement and ultimately comes into conflict with international privacy rights and sovereignty. The CLOUD Act, both a tool and a challenge, highlights the intricate, often conflicting web of international law in the digital age. It's a narrative of ambition and compromise, clarity and confusion, cooperation and contention.

The challenge ahead lies in untangling these threads, fostering harmony where there is discord, and navigating the delicate balance between the needs of law enforcement, the rights of individuals, and the sovereignty of nations. The implications of CLOUD versus GDPR remain unfinished, with global observers closely tracking the next phase of events as the narrative continues to evolve.

Case Study: The Australian Legal and Regulatory Framework

The Internet's inherent interconnectivity calls for a comprehensive and coordinated approach to security, as exemplified by the Australian experience. The Australian approach serves as a case study that emphasizes the principles of cooperation, balance, and transparency and offers insights into the multifaceted nature of cybersecurity.

Inspired by the United States, Australia created an 'Emergency Response Team' within the Signals Directorate of the Defence Department. This organization played a vital role in defending against cyberattacks and other malicious activities and promoting international cooperation.

However, early progress had challenges. The government's over-reliance on military and intelligence agencies led to underinvestment in civilian organizations. This imbalance demonstrated the need for a diversified cybersecurity approach catering to both civilian and military sectors.

Managing sensitive information is crucial for national security. Australia initially took a controlled approach, guarding information through intelligence agencies and legislation.

The introduction of the Freedom of Information Act marked a shift, enabling greater public access to certain government documents and increased transparency.

Recently, Australia has further eased national security controls on information and communication.

The key legislative components in the Australian context are:

Australian Privacy Principles (APPs)–APPs are an amendment to the Privacy Act 1988 (Cth), which aims to end the complexity and confusion in the application of privacy laws by creating a set of APPs (principles) that will apply to both federal government agencies and the private sector. These principles (APPs) are intended to regulate:

- The collection
- Holding
- Use, and
- Disclosure of personal information that is included in records

They apply to government agencies and private organizations having more than AUD$3 million in annual turnover.

Cybercrime Act: This act offers comprehensive regulation of computer and Internet-related offenses, such as unlawful access and computer trespass, damaging data and impeding access to computers, theft of data, computer fraud, cyberstalking harassment, and possession of child pornography.

The Cybercrime Act makes the following offenses illegal (s.477.1 to s.478.4):

- Unauthorized access, modification, or impairment to commit a serious offense

- Unauthorized impairment of data to cause impairment

- Unauthorized impairment of electronic communications

- Possession of data with intent to commit a computer offense

- Supply of data with intent to commit a computer offense

- Unauthorized access to restricted data

- Unauthorized impairment of data held in a computer disk, credit card, etc.

Spam Act: This act established a scheme for regulating commercial email and other types of electronic messages. It restricts unauthorized, unsolicited electronic messages with some exceptions. This act is regulated by the "Australian Communications and Media Authority."

The full definition of Spam is "the sending of unsolicited commercial messages via email, SMS, MMS, and instant message either within Australia or to a device connected to an Australian service provider.

The three main rules of the Spam Act are:

- **Consent**: Only send commercial electronic messages with the addressee's consent, either express or inferred

- **Identification**: Include clear and accurate information about the person or business that is responsible for sending the commercial message

- **Unsubscribe**: Ensure that a functional unsubscribe facility is included in all commercial electronic messages and deal with unsubscribe requests promptly

Telecommunications (Interception and Access) Act: The primary objective of this act is to protect the privacy of individuals who use Australian telecommunication systems. Another purpose is to specify the circumstances under which it is lawful for interception of, or access to, communications to take place. This act covers both stored and real-time communications.

The Privacy Act in Australia defines obligations for entities known as 'APP entities.' These include federal government agencies and a broad range of organizations like individuals, businesses, partnerships, and trusts. However, some entities are exempt, such as small businesses with an annual turnover under $3 million, registered political parties, and state or territory authorities.

Notably, even small business operators may fall under the Act in certain cases, for example, if they have another business earning over $3 million, deal with health services or personal information, work under Commonwealth contracts, or operate as a credit reporting body.

The Act contains 13 Australian Privacy Principles (APPs) which dictate how personal information should be managed–collected, used, disclosed, and stored. There are specific provisions for credit reporting that entities dealing with credit-related information must observe. APP entities must also adhere to an 'APP code,' a written code of practice that gives further guidelines on managing personal information specific to different entities or industries, such as the Credit Reporting Code (CR Code).

Understanding these regulations is crucial for all executives, project managers, and business analysts to ensure that any system they build or manage complies with the legal requirements for handling personal information, including following the APPs, credit reporting provisions, and any relevant APP codes. We will discuss each of the thirteen Australian privacy principles and, in particular, look at what you need to know as a project manager or business analyst.

Australian Privacy Principle (APP) 1: deals with the open and transparent management of personal information under the Privacy Act:

- **Establishing Privacy Practices:** Every organization is required to develop practices, procedures, and systems that ensure adherence to all Australian Privacy Principles. This includes establishing efficient ways to handle privacy-related inquiries and complaints.

- **Privacy Policy Development and Accessibility:** Organizations must create a clear, accessible privacy policy detailing their personal information management. This policy should be easily available to anyone interacting with the entity, typically through the entity's website.

- **Implementing Reasonable Measures:** you must take reasonable steps to implement systems that protect personal information privacy, considering the specific functions and activities.

- **Privacy Policy Maintenance:** The privacy policy must be well-articulated, current, and reflective of the entity's latest privacy practices and procedures.

- **Privacy Policy Contents:** The policy must clearly state:

  o Types of personal information collected and held

  o Methods of collection and storage

  o Purposes of collecting, holding, using, and disclosing personal information

  o Procedures for individuals to access and correct their information

  o Complaint lodging process concerning privacy principle breaches and the entity's response mechanism

  o Potential disclosure of personal information to overseas recipients, including the countries where these recipients might be located, if practical to specify.

- **Accessibility of Privacy Policy:** Entities must ensure their privacy policy is readily available, free of charge, and in a format suitable for their audience.

- **Common Practice for Accessibility:** It's a common practice for entities to make their privacy policy accessible via their website, ensuring easy public access.

- **Responding to Requests for the Privacy Policy:** If an individual or organization requests the privacy policy in a specific format, the entity must reasonably accommodate this request.

It is clear, from statements made by the ASIC Commissioner and the actions taken by regulators in Australia and overseas, that having an effective plan is an essential undertaking. When your organization gets hacked (and it will), if you cannot produce a working Privacy Policy, it will raise grave concerns with regulators and the courts and might result in action taken against individuals.

Australian Privacy Principle (APP) 2: part of the Privacy Act, focuses on the rights of individuals to remain anonymous or use a pseudonym in their interactions with organizations. This principle is crucial for non-technical managers to understand, as it directly impacts how organizations interact with individuals while respecting their privacy preferences:

- **Right to Anonymity or Pseudonym:** APP 2 guarantees that individuals can choose to either remain anonymous or use a pseudonym when dealing with an organization. This choice is available unless specific circumstances make it impractical or if the law mandates identification.

- **Option of Non-Identification:** When individuals engage with an organization, they should be offered the option to not disclose their identity or use a pseudonym. This approach safeguards the individual's privacy and personal information.

- **Exceptions to the Rule:** There are two main exceptions to this principle:

  o **Legal Obligations:** If an Australian law, court, or tribunal order requires the organization to interact with identified individuals, the option of anonymity or pseudonymity is not applicable.

  o **Practicality Concerns:** If it is impractical for the organization to deal with unidentified individuals or those using a pseudonym, they are not required to offer this option. "Impractical" here refers to situations where the entity's operations or obligations cannot be reasonably fulfilled without knowing the individual's identity.

In essence, APP 2 strongly emphasizes respecting an individual's preference for privacy through anonymity or pseudonymity. APP entities are expected to uphold this principle, providing the option of non-identification whenever feasible, unless legal requirements or practical limitations necessitate otherwise. This principle plays a significant role in promoting privacy and personal information control within the framework of the Privacy Act.

Australian Privacy Principle (APP) 3: an essential component of the Privacy Act, governs the collection of personal information by organizations. This principle is particularly relevant for managers who need to understand the proper ways of collecting personal information:

- **Necessity of Collection:** you are only allowed to collect personal information if it's reasonably necessary for your business functions or activities. This means the information should be directly relevant and crucial for the operations you manage.

- **Direct Collection from Individuals:** Personal information should ideally be gathered directly from the individuals concerned, unless it's impractical or a specific legal exception applies. This practice ensures transparency and gives individuals control over their data.

- **Consent for Sensitive Information:** Collecting sensitive information, like health records or political opinions, requires the individual's consent, barring certain legal exceptions. Sensitive information demands a higher level of privacy protection.

- **Government Agencies' Collection Criteria:** Government agencies must ensure that any personal information (other than sensitive information) they collect is strictly necessary for, or directly related to, their functions or activities.

- **Organizations' Collection Criteria:** For businesses, the collection of personal information is permissible only if it's necessary for one or more of their functions or activities.

- **Lawful and Fair Collection Practices:** The collection of personal information must be conducted lawfully and fairly. This means adhering to legal standards and ensuring equitable treatment of individuals during the collection process.

Exceptions to Direct Collection:

- For government agencies, exceptions include situations where the individual consents to having their information collected from another source, or when required or authorized by law or a court/tribunal order.

- In cases where direct collection from the individual is unreasonable or impractical, entities may collect information from alternative sources.

By adhering to APP 3, organizations are committed to collecting personal information responsibly, ensuring it's necessary for their operations, obtained directly from individuals when feasible, with proper consent for sensitive data, and through legal and fair methods. This approach upholds privacy standards and fosters a responsible environment for handling personal information within organizations.

Australian Privacy Principle (APP) 4: a crucial part of the Privacy Act, guides organizations on how to manage unsolicited personal information. In a clear and authoritative narrative, here's what managers need to know:

- **Assessment of Lawfulness:** When an organization receives personal information it did not solicit, it must first assess whether it could have legally collected that information under APP 3. This means evaluating if the information could have been lawfully obtained if the organization had sought it.

- **Compliance with Other APPs:** If the organization concludes that it could have lawfully collected the information under APP 3, it must ensure compliance with all the other Australian Privacy Principles. This is to maintain a standard of privacy and protection in line with established guidelines.

- **Destruction or De-identification:** Conversely, if the organization determines that it would not have been lawful to collect the information under APP 3, it must either destroy the information or de-identify it. This action should be taken as long as it is legal and reasonable.

- **Timely Determination:** The organization is required to make this assessment within a reasonable timeframe after receiving the unsolicited information. This prompt evaluation is crucial to ensure compliance with privacy regulations.

- **Use or Disclosure for Assessment:** To aid in this determination process, the organization is permitted to use or disclose the unsolicited personal information, but solely for the purpose of making this assessment.

- **Handling Non-Lawful Information:** If the organization finds that it could not have lawfully collected the unsolicited information and it's not part of a government record, it must, as soon as feasibly possible, either destroy the information or ensure it is de-identified, provided this is legally and reasonably feasible.

- **Treatment as Collected Information:** If none of the conditions for destruction or de-identification apply, the organization must treat the unsolicited personal information as if it were collected under APP 3. This means adhering to Australian Privacy Principles 5 to 13, which cover aspects like use, storage, and security of the information.

In summary, APP 4 mandates that organizations handle unsolicited personal information with the same level of care and legality as solicited information, ensuring privacy and protection standards are upheld. This involves timely assessment, compliance with privacy principles, and appropriate actions like destruction or de-identification when necessary.

Australian Privacy Principle (APP) 5: an integral part of the Privacy Act, sets out the obligations for organizations in notifying individuals about the collection of personal information. This principle is key for ensuring transparency and informed consent in the handling of personal data:

- **Notification of Key Details:** When collecting personal information, an organization is required to inform individuals about certain critical aspects. This includes whether the information is sourced from third parties, the purposes of collection, potential recipients, and how individuals can access, correct, or raise concerns about their information.

- **Use of Collection Statements:** A common method to comply with APP 5 is through "collection statements" presented alongside forms or materials used for gathering personal information. These statements usually refer to or link to the entity's privacy policy.

- **Timing of Notification:** you must notify individuals at or before the time of collection, or as soon as feasible afterwards. It's crucial that individuals are made aware of the relevant details at the earliest opportunity.

- **Comprehensive Notification Content:** The notification must cover the entity's identity and contact details, acknowledgment if the information is collected from third parties or if the individual may be unaware of the collection, legal bases for collection, the purposes of collection, potential consequences of non-collection, usual recipients of the information, access and correction facilities, complaint procedures, and possible overseas disclosures, including the countries of such recipients if practicable.

By adhering to APP 5, entities ensure that individuals are well-informed about how their personal information is collected, used, and managed. This principle is fundamental in establishing a transparent relationship between entities and individuals, fostering trust, and enabling individuals to exercise their rights effectively in relation to their personal information. It's a critical step in ensuring entities act responsibly and accountably in the realm of personal data management.

Australian Privacy Principle (APP) 6: addresses the use or disclosure of personal information by organizations. It is crucial for non-technical managers to understand how this principle guides the handling of personal data within their organizations:

- **Restrictions on Use or Disclosure:** APP 6 primarily restricts organizations from using or disclosing personal information for purposes other than the original reason for which it was collected. However, there are conditions under which this information can be used for secondary purposes. These include situations where the individual has consented, where the individual would reasonably expect their information to be used for a related secondary purpose, or where specific legal exceptions apply.

- **Prescribed Exceptions:** There are notable exceptions where the use or disclosure of personal information is permissible. These exceptions usually relate to scenarios where it is necessary to protect someone's health or safety or when it is in the public interest.

- **Conditions for Secondary Use or Disclosure:** If an organization holds personal information that was collected for a specific purpose, it cannot use or disclose this information for a different purpose unless it obtains the individual's consent or if specific conditions, as outlined in subclauses 6.2 or 6.3, are met.

- **Subclause 6.2 Conditions:** These conditions apply if the individual reasonably expects the organization to use or disclose their information for a secondary purpose. The secondary purpose must be directly related to the primary purpose for sensitive information or the primary purpose for non-sensitive information. Additional conditions include compliance with Australian law or court orders, the existence of permitted general or health situations, or if the use or disclosure is deemed necessary for enforcement-related activities by an enforcement body.

- **Record-Keeping for Health Situations:** When an organization uses or discloses personal information in accordance with permitted health situations, it must make a written note of such use or disclosure.

In summary, APP 6 establishes that organizations must handle personal information responsibly, with strict guidelines on its use or disclosure. This principle ensures that personal information is not used or shared beyond its original collection purpose without proper consent or justification, thus safeguarding individual privacy and maintaining trust between organizations and the individuals whose data they handle.

Australian Privacy Principle (APP) 7: provides specific guidelines on using personal information for direct marketing by organizations. This principle is vital for non-technical managers to comprehend, as it delineates the circumstances under which personal information can be utilized for marketing purposes:

- **General Prohibition with Conditions:** APP 7 sets a default rule that organizations are generally not allowed to use personal information for direct marketing. However, there are exceptions to this rule. These exceptions include situations where the individual would reasonably expect their information to be used for direct marketing purposes or where they have explicitly consented to it. Additionally, organizations must have an 'opt-out' mechanism in place, allowing individuals to choose not to receive direct marketing communications. This option should be available unless the individual has previously requested to opt out.

- **Conditions for Use or Disclosure in Direct Marketing:** Despite the general prohibition, there are specific conditions under which an organization may use or disclose personal information for direct marketing purposes. These conditions include:

o   The personal information must have been collected directly from the individual.

o   The individual would reasonably expect their information to be used or disclosed for direct marketing by the organization.

o   The organization must provide a simple and accessible method for individuals to request not to receive direct marketing communications.

o   The individual should not have already requested the organization to stop receiving direct marketing communications.

In essence, APP 7 emphasizes the importance of respecting individuals' expectations and choices regarding the use of their personal information for marketing purposes. It ensures that personal data is not used for direct marketing without appropriate consent or reasonable expectation, and that individuals have a clear and easy way to opt out of such marketing communications. This principle aligns with the broader objectives of the Privacy Act to protect individual privacy while allowing for legitimate business practices.

Australian Privacy Principle (APP) 8: regulates the cross-border disclosure of personal information by organizations. It's essential to understand the responsibilities and conditions associated with transferring personal data overseas:

- **Ensuring Compliance with APPs:** APP 8 obliges organizations to take reasonable steps to ensure that any personal information disclosed to recipients overseas does not result in a breach of the Australian Privacy Principles. This often involves imposing contractual obligations on the overseas recipient to uphold the standards of the APPs.

- **Liability for Breaches by Overseas Recipients:** If the overseas recipient violates the APPs, the disclosing organization is held liable under the Privacy Act for that breach. This highlights the importance of due diligence and accountability in international data transfers.

Preconditions for Disclosure: Before disclosing personal information to an overseas recipient who is not part of the organization or the individual, reasonable steps must be taken to ensure the recipient adheres to the Australian Privacy Principles in relation to that information.

Detailed Exceptions to Subclause 8.1: Specific conditions under which subclause 8.1 does not apply include:

- The organization reasonably believes the recipient is subject to a law or scheme with substantially similar protections as the APPs, with enforceable mechanisms for the individual.

- The individual explicitly consents to the disclosure, being informed that their consent negates the applicability of subclause 8.1.

- The disclosure is required or authorized by Australian law or a court/tribunal order.

- A permitted general situation exists regarding the disclosure.

- For agencies, if the disclosure is required or authorized by an international agreement on information sharing to which Australia is a party, or if it is necessary for enforcement activities and the recipient performs similar functions to an enforcement body.

In essence, APP 8 mandates organizations to be vigilant in ensuring overseas data transfers comply with privacy principles akin to those in Australia, except under specific conditions. This principle underscores the importance of protecting personal information in a global context, maintaining accountability and offering individuals reassurances about the safety of their data when it crosses borders.

Australian Privacy Principle (APP) 9: sets specific restrictions on how organizations handle government-related identifiers. Understanding this principle is essential for managers to ensure compliance with privacy laws:

Restrictions on Government-Related Identifiers: APP 9 explicitly prohibits organizations from adopting, using, or disclosing a government-related identifier of an individual as their own identifier unless certain conditions are met. These conditions include:

- The use or disclosure of the identifier is required or authorized by law.

- The organization uses or discloses the identifier to verify the identity of the individual.

- The use or disclosure falls under another exception prescribed by law.

Definition of Government-Related Identifiers: Government-related identifiers are unique numbers or codes assigned to individuals by government agencies. These can include an array of identifiers such as an individual's driver's license number, Medicare number, passport number, and tax file number. These identifiers are often sensitive and integral to an individual's identity and interactions with government services.

The application of APP 9 is vital in managing the use of government-related identifiers. It ensures that these identifiers, which are pivotal to the government's interaction with individuals, are not misused by other entities for their own purposes. By adhering to this principle, organizations contribute to safeguarding individuals' privacy and preventing potential identity fraud or misuse of government-issued identifiers. This compliance forms a part of the broader responsibility of organizations to handle personal information ethically and legally.

Australian Privacy Principle (APP) 10: focuses on the quality of personal information that organizations collect, use, disclose, and hold. For managers, it's crucial to understand and implement the requirements of this principle to ensure the integrity and reliability of personal data:

- **Ensuring Accuracy and Relevance:** APP 10 obligates organizations to ensure that the personal information they deal with is accurate, complete, and up-to-date. This requirement is particularly important when it comes to using or disclosing personal information. The principle underscores that personal information should only be used or disclosed if it is relevant to the purpose of such use or disclosure.

- **Responsibility in Collection:** The principle requires organizations to take reasonable steps, considering the circumstances, to ensure that the personal information they collect is accurate, current, and complete. This means actively verifying and updating information as needed, especially when it is to be used for critical decisions affecting individuals.

- **Ensuring Quality in Use and Disclosure:** Similarly, when it comes to using or disclosing personal information, organizations must take reasonable measures to ensure that the data is not just accurate and current, but also complete and relevant for the intended purpose. This aspect of APP 10 emphasizes the need for ongoing diligence in handling personal information throughout its lifecycle within the organization.

In essence, APP 10 establishes a standard for the quality of personal information within organizations, ensuring that data handling processes do not compromise the accuracy, completeness, or relevance of personal information. This is key to maintaining trust and integrity in organizational practices, especially in activities that involve personal data. Compliance with APP 10 is not just a legal obligation but also a fundamental aspect of responsible data management.

Australian Privacy Principle (APP) 11: outlines the responsibilities of organizations regarding the security of personal information. For managers, understanding and implementing this principle is essential for safeguarding personal data:

- **Obligation to Protect Personal Information:** APP 11 imposes a duty on organizations to take reasonable steps to protect personal information from a range of threats, including misuse, interference, loss, unauthorized access, modification, or disclosure. This means implementing appropriate security measures that correspond to the nature of the information and the potential risks to its integrity and confidentiality.

- **Destruction or De-identification of Unnecessary Information:** Beyond just protecting information, the principle also requires organizations to responsibly dispose of or de-identify personal information that is no longer needed for any purpose permitted under the relevant regulations. This step is crucial unless a legal requirement exists to retain the information, in which case it must be securely stored.

- **Comprehensive Security Measures:** The principle emphasizes the need for comprehensive measures to protect personal information. These measures should be suitable for the specific circumstances of the organization and should cover all aspects of information security, including physical, digital, and procedural safeguards.

- **Conditions for Disposal or De-identification:** If an organization holds personal information that is no longer needed, is not part of a Commonwealth record, and is not required to be retained by law or a court/tribunal order, it must take reasonable steps to either securely destroy the information or ensure that it is de-identified. This ensures that personal information is not left vulnerable to security breaches once it has served its purpose.

In summary, APP 11 underscores the critical responsibility of organizations in maintaining the security of personal information. This includes not only protecting data from various forms of compromise, but also ensuring that it is appropriately destroyed or de-identified when it is no longer required. Adherence to this principle is vital for maintaining the trust of individuals and upholding the organization's reputation, as well as complying with legal obligations regarding data security.

Australian Privacy Principle (APP) 12: outlines the right of individuals to access their personal information held by organizations. This principle is crucial for managers to understand as it directly relates to transparency and individuals' rights over their data:

- **Right to Access Personal Information:** APP 12 establishes that organizations are required to provide individuals with access to their personal information upon request. This principle empowers individuals to be informed about the data held about them, promoting transparency and accountability.

- **Exceptions for Government Agencies:** If your organization is a government agency, there are specific instances where it may be authorized or obligated to refuse access to personal information. This is particularly relevant when the refusal is in line with the Freedom of Information Act or other similar Commonwealth Acts or Norfolk Island enactments. In such cases, the agency is not required to provide access in accordance with clause 12.1 of APP 12.

- **Conditions for Refusal by Non-Government Agencies:** For non-government organizations, certain conditions may justify the refusal to provide access to personal information. These include situations where:

  - Granting access would pose a serious threat to the life, health, or safety of any individual, or to public health or safety.

  - Access would unreasonably impact the privacy of others.

  - The request for access is frivolous or vexatious.

o   The information relates to ongoing or
    anticipated legal proceedings, and would
    not be accessible through discovery.

o   Access would reveal the intentions of the
    organization in negotiations in a way that
    prejudices those negotiations.

o   Granting access would be unlawful, or
    denying access is required or authorized by
    law or a court/tribunal order.

o   There is suspicion of unlawful activity or
    misconduct related to the organization's
    functions or activities, and access would
    likely undermine actions related to this
    matter.

o   Access would reveal evaluative information
    generated within the organization in a
    commercially sensitive decision-making
    process.

In summary, APP 12 ensures that individuals have the right
to access their personal information held by organizations,
fostering an environment of transparency and respect for
privacy rights. However, this access is not absolute and can
be limited under certain conditions, especially where
access might compromise legal proceedings, privacy, or
public safety. Organizations must balance these
considerations carefully to comply with APP 12 while
respecting the rights and safety of individuals and the
community.

Australian Privacy Principle (APP) 13: focuses on correcting personal information held by organizations. It is a critical aspect for managers to understand, as it involves ensuring the accuracy and relevance of personal data:

- **Obligation to Correct Personal Information:** APP 13 places an obligation on organizations to take reasonable steps to correct personal information they hold. This correction should occur either when an individual specifically requests it or when the organization itself recognizes that the information is inaccurate, outdated, incomplete, irrelevant, or misleading. The correction process must consider the purpose for which the information is held, emphasizing the importance of maintaining current and relevant data.

- **Handling Refusal of Correction Requests:** If an organization decides to refuse a correction request, it must clearly communicate the reasons for this refusal to the individual. In some situations, the organization may also be required to attach a statement from the individual to the personal information. This statement would indicate that the individual believes the information to be incorrect, ensuring their perspective is recorded.

- **Notifying Third Parties of Corrections:** Once a correction is made to personal information, the organization might need to notify third parties who previously received the incorrect information. This step is crucial to ensure that all relevant parties have the most current and accurate data.

In summary, APP 13 underscores the responsibility of organizations to actively manage the accuracy and completeness of personal information. This includes responding to correction requests, providing reasons for any refusal, and communicating corrections to third parties as necessary. By adhering to this principle, organizations can enhance the integrity of the personal information they manage and maintain trust with individuals whose data they hold. Compliance with APP 13 is not only a legal requirement but also a key aspect of responsible data stewardship.

Proposed Changes to Privacy Principles

The European Union's General Data Protection Regulation (GDPR) is often hailed as the global benchmark for data protection and privacy laws. While Australia's Privacy Act 1988 offers substantial privacy measures, it hasn't quite reached the GDPR's level of personal information protection. Recognizing this, the Australian Attorney-General has put forward significant reforms to bolster the country's privacy laws, as detailed in the Privacy Act Review Report. In September 2023, the Federal Government responded to these proposals, committing to 38 directly, agreeing in principle to another 68 pending further discussion and analysis, and noting 10 for future consideration.

This commitment signals a major overhaul on the horizon, with the Government planning to introduce new legislation in 2024. These changes aim to narrow the gap between Australia's privacy standards and those of the GDPR, though how closely the two will align remains to be seen. Our analysis in this two-part series begins with exploring key proposed changes, including defining roles such as 'controllers 'and 'processors 'within the Privacy Act, refining exemptions, and enhancing the Notifiable Data Breaches Scheme. The upcoming reforms could significantly impact how personal data is managed, particularly for entities that process data on behalf of others, marking a shift towards greater accountability and protection in line with global standards.

The 2023 survey by the Office of the Australian Information Commissioner (OAIC) reveals a significant concern among Australians regarding the safety of their personal data. With 62% of respondents expressing worry over protecting their information and 75% viewing data breaches as a major risk—an increase of 13% since 2020—it's clear that data privacy has become a critical issue. However, only a small fraction (32%) feel they have adequate control over their data privacy, prompting a call for stronger legislative measures and personal data control.

In response to these concerns, the Privacy Act Review Report, following two years of comprehensive discussions, advocates for substantial updates to Australia's privacy laws to align with the expectations of the digital era. This includes enhancing legal safeguards against unauthorized use of data and ensuring personal information is securely managed to counteract identity theft and scams, which are vital for maintaining Australian businesses' trustworthiness and international standing.

Recognizing the urgency, the government has committed to refining privacy protections to foster digital innovation and safeguard against risks. The key reforms agreed upon by the Government encompass several critical areas:

- **Security and Destruction of Personal Information:** The reforms aim to bolster the security of personal data by clarifying the obligations of entities to take reasonable steps that include both technical and organizational measures. This measure is particularly significant in an era where data breaches are becoming increasingly sophisticated. The Office of the Australian Information Commissioner (OAIC) is set to provide further guidance on what constitutes reasonable steps, leveraging technical insights from the Australian Cybersecurity Centre. This guidance is anticipated to help entities better navigate their data protection responsibilities.

- **Automated Decision-Making:** Another significant area of reform is the requirement for privacy policies to explicitly outline how personal information is utilized in automated decisions that significantly impact individuals. This change addresses growing concerns about the transparency and accountability of algorithms and automated systems in decision-making processes affecting individuals' rights and freedoms.

- **Children's Privacy:** Recognizing the vulnerability of children in the digital space, the Government plans to introduce a Children's Online Privacy Code. This code will apply to online services likely accessed by children, defining 'child' as any individual under the age of 18. This reform represents a proactive step towards safeguarding children's privacy online, ensuring that digital services adhere to standards that protect young users.

- **Enforcement:** Perhaps one of the most consequential aspects of the proposed reforms is the introduction of new tiers of civil penalty provisions. This includes a mid-tier for privacy interferences lacking a "serious" element and low-level provisions for administrative breaches. Furthermore, the reforms propose to expand the courts' powers in making orders following established privacy interferences and empower the Commissioner to require entities to address and mitigate individual losses due to privacy breaches. Additionally, the Information Commissioner is set to receive broader investigative powers and the authority to conduct public inquiries and reviews, significantly enhancing the enforcement framework.

These reforms, agreed upon by the Government, are pivotal for empowering individuals, protecting minors, and ensuring businesses can operate securely and competitively in a global landscape, all while navigating the balance between innovation and privacy.

The Australian Government is taking steps to enhance data protection and privacy laws, drawing inspiration from the European Union's General Data Protection Regulation (GDPR), considered the benchmark for privacy regulation. Notably, the Privacy Act Review Report has highlighted areas for significant reform, with the Government committing to a series of proposals aimed at strengthening Australia's privacy framework.

One key area of reform is the small business exemption under the current Privacy Act, which exempts small businesses with less than $3 million AUD in annual turnover from compliance. Given the growing privacy risks, the Report suggests reevaluating this exemption to ensure small businesses also adhere to robust privacy standards, aligning more closely with the GDPR's approach. However, this change would come after thorough impact analysis and consultation to gauge the potential effects on small businesses and develop supportive guidelines.

Another focal point is the employee records exemption, which currently allows private sector employers to manage employee records without full adherence to the Privacy Act. The Report recommends not removing this exemption entirely but enhancing privacy protections for employees through consultations, balancing the need for businesses to collect employee data with privacy considerations.

The journalism exemption is also under review, with proposals suggesting media organizations maintain higher standards of personal information security, including mandatory reporting of data breaches. This aligns with the GDPR's flexible approach, allowing Member States to balance data protection with journalistic freedom.

Regarding data breach notifications, the Report proposes aligning the Notifiable Data Breaches (NDB) scheme more closely with the GDPR, particularly by introducing a more stringent timeframe for reporting breaches. Currently, entities have 30 days to assess a suspected breach, but the proposed reforms suggest a 72-hour notification period once a breach is confirmed, enhancing promptness and transparency in response to data breaches.

These reforms reflect a commitment to updating Australia's privacy laws to better protect individuals' personal information in the digital age, balancing innovation with privacy and security needs. For non-technical managers and board members, staying informed about these impending changes is crucial to ensure compliance and safeguard against privacy risks.

The Australian Government's response to the Attorney-General's Privacy Act Review Report signifies a pivotal moment in the evolution of Australia's data protection landscape. This response, published on 28 September 2023 after comprehensive public consultation, underscores a strong commitment to modernizing privacy legislation, aligning it more closely with the stringent global standards epitomized by frameworks such as the European Union's General Data Protection Regulation (GDPR).

These proposed changes signify a robust effort by the Australian Government to uplift the country's privacy protections, ensuring they are fit for the challenges of the digital age. By introducing these legislative amendments in 2024, the Government aims to protect individuals' privacy more effectively and maintain Australia's standing in the international business community by ensuring its privacy laws meet global standards. For businesses and organizations, this heralds a period of adjustment and heightened responsibility in collecting, using, and safeguarding personal information.

The Australian Government's proactive steps towards reforming the Privacy Act, as detailed in the Attorney-General's Privacy Act Review Report, aim to align the country's privacy protections more closely with international standards, notably those set by the European Union's General Data Protection Regulation (GDPR). With the government agreeing to or agreeing in principle to a majority of the proposed changes, the focus is on enhancing data protection through measures such as eliminating exemptions for small businesses, extending protections to private sector employees, refining the consent mechanism, and ensuring fairness in the handling of personal data. These reforms underscore Australia's commitment to bolstering privacy in the digital age, highlighting the balance between safeguarding individual rights and fostering digital innovation. The proposed introduction of concepts like 'controllers' and 'processors', alongside updates to the Notifiable Data Breaches Scheme and new provisions for overseas data transfers, mark significant steps towards a more comprehensive and stringent privacy regime. As the government gears up to introduce these legislative changes in 2024, the emphasis is on creating a more secure and trustworthy digital environment that aligns with global privacy standards, aiming to protect individuals from emerging digital risks while ensuring Australia's competitiveness on the international stage.

The Perfect Storm

The Australian government's reforms to the **Security of Critical Infrastructure Act 2018 (SOCI Act)** have introduced a new **Enhanced Cybersecurity Obligation**

(ECSO) framework that applies to the nation's most critical infrastructure assets, known as **Systems of National Significance (SoNS)**. This framework is designed to bolster the cybersecurity resilience of these vital assets and ensure they have comprehensive, regularly tested plans to effectively prepare for, respond to, and mitigate the impact of cyberattacks.

The ECSO framework comprises four key components: cyber incident response planning, cybersecurity exercises, vulnerability assessments, and system information sharing. Each plays a crucial role in enhancing the overall cybersecurity posture of SoNS assets.

Firstly, the ECSO mandates that entities responsible for SoNS assets develop and maintain detailed cyber incident response plans. These plans should outline the steps and procedures to be followed during a cybersecurity incident, ensuring a swift and coordinated response to minimize the impact on the asset and its dependent systems. Regular reviews and updates of these plans are required to keep pace with the evolving threat landscape.

Secondly, SoNS entities are required to conduct regular cybersecurity exercises to test the effectiveness of their incident response plans and overall cyber resilience. These exercises can range from discussion-based activities to full-scale simulations of cyberattacks, allowing entities to identify potential weaknesses and areas for improvement in their response capabilities. The government will work closely with each entity to determine the most appropriate type and frequency of exercises based on factors such as the nature of the asset, its sector, and the current threat environment.

Thirdly, the ECSO framework requires SoNS entities to undertake periodic vulnerability assessments to proactively identify and address security gaps that malicious actors could exploit. These assessments may include system design reviews, hands-on penetration testing, or automated vulnerability scans. The government has the authority to direct an entity to conduct an evaluation and, if necessary, to authorize an official to perform the assessment on the entity's behalf. The results of these assessments must be documented in a vulnerability assessment report and shared with the government.

Lastly, to support the development of a national-level, real-time threat picture, SoNS entities are obligated to share specified system information, such as logs and event data, with the government. This information sharing enables the government to analyze trends, identify emerging threats, and disseminate actionable intelligence back to the entities, ultimately strengthening the collective defense of Australia's critical infrastructure. The government may request this information periodically or in response to specific events and, in some cases, may require software installation to facilitate automated reporting.

The industries subject to the SOCI Act and the ECSO framework include:

- Communications
- Energy
- Water and Sewerage
- Transport
- Food and Grocery
- Health

- Banking and Finance
- Space technology
- Defense industry
- Higher Education and Research
- Data Storage or Processing

The inclusion of these sectors highlights the wide-ranging impact and interdependencies of critical infrastructure assets on the nation's economic and social well-being and national security. By implementing the ECSO framework, the Australian government aims to ensure that the most critical assets within these sectors are well-prepared to withstand and respond to cyber threats, thereby maintaining the continuity of essential services and protecting the nation's interests.

Key Impacts:

- SoNS assets are now subject to ECSO on top of pre-existing security obligations.

- The Secretary of Home Affairs determines which specific ECSO applies to each SoNS.

- SoNS entities must develop and maintain detailed cyber incident response plans.

- Regular cybersecurity exercises must be conducted to test response capabilities.

- Entities must undergo vulnerability assessments to identify and address security gaps.

- System information must be provided to the government to enable real-time threat monitoring.

Core Recommendations:

- Determine whether your critical infrastructure assets have been declared SoNS and understand applicable ECSO

- Develop or update cyber incident response plans in line with new requirements

- Plan and conduct comprehensive annual cyber exercises to test response plans rigorously

- Produce thorough post-exercise evaluation reports assessing strengths and improvement areas

- Implement a vulnerability management program to identify and remediate vulnerabilities proactively

- Implement technical and process changes to meet system information-sharing obligations

- Engage leadership to ensure awareness and appropriate resourcing to meet ECSO requirements

---

Background on SoNS

The SOCI Act reforms introduce the **Systems of National Significance (SoNS)** concept — a subset of critical infrastructure assets deemed to be of the highest criticality to the nation. The Minister for Home Affairs can privately declare an asset as SoNS based on factors such as interdependencies with other critical infrastructure and the severity of consequences if it is disrupted. SoNS assets are subject to the new ECSO and existing security obligations.

Overview of Enhanced Cybersecurity Obligations

The ECSO framework includes four key components that can be selectively applied to SoNS assets:

1. **Cyber Incident Response Plans**–SoNS entities must develop, maintain, and comply with detailed plans outlining how to respond to and mitigate cybersecurity incidents affecting their assets. While no specific template is mandated, plans should align with the entity's operating environment and threat profile and be regularly reviewed.

2. **Cybersecurity Exercises**–Entities must conduct practical exercises to test their incident response plans and overall cyber resilience. Exercise formats can include discussion-based activities or functional simulations. The government will work with each entity to determine appropriate exercises based on sector and threat factors. After each workout, entities must provide an evaluation report assessing outcomes and identifying improvement opportunities.

3. **Vulnerability Assessments**–SoNS entities must undergo vulnerability assessments to identify security gaps that malicious actors could exploit

proactively. Assessments may include design reviews, hands-on testing, or automated scans. The government can direct an entity to conduct an evaluation and authorize an official to perform it if it is not completed. Results must be provided in a vulnerability assessment report.

4. **Provision of System Information**–To support whole-of-nation threat awareness, SoNS entities must provide government-specified system information (e.g., logs, event data). This enables the development of a real-time threat picture to share actionable intelligence and uplift collective defense. Information can be requested on a periodic or event-driven basis. In limited cases, the government may require software installation to enable reporting.

Supporting guidance has been published to help SoNS entities conduct practical cyber exercises aligned with the obligations. This includes advice on exercise scenario development, incident response plan testing, participant involvement, and post-exercise reporting and improvement planning.

A series of critical compliance and reporting dates have accompanied the SOCI Act reforms and the introduction of the ECSO framework. These dates are designed to provide a phased approach to implementing the new obligations, giving entities sufficient time to assess their status, understand the requirements, and implement the necessary measures.

Key dates for compliance and reporting include:

- **The Mandatory Cyber Incident Notification** obligation (Part 2B of the SOCI Act) came into effect for most critical infrastructure assets. Entities had until July 8, 2022, to comply with this obligation, which required them to report critical cybersecurity incidents within 12 hours and other cybersecurity incidents within 72 hours of becoming aware of the incident.

- **Register of Critical Assets:** The six-month grace period for compliance with the Register of Critical Infrastructure Assets (Part 2 of the SOCI Act) concluded. Entities had until October 2022 to provide the required operational and ownership information to the Register.

- **SOCI 'turned on':** The Security of Critical Infrastructure (Critical infrastructure risk management program) Rules (LIN 23/006) 2023 (CIRMP Rules) came into effect, "switching on" the Risk Management Program obligation (Part 2A of the SOCI Act) for 13 critical infrastructure asset classes. The AusCheck Legislation Amendment (Critical Infrastructure Background Check) Regulations 2023 also commenced in February 2023.

- **Grace Period:** The six-month grace period for compliance with the Risk Management Program obligation (Part 2A of the SOCI Act) has concluded. Entities had until August 2023 to establish and comply with their risk management programs.

- **Cyber Frameworks Grace Period:** The 12-month grace period for compliance with the cyber and information security framework requirements under sections 8(4) and 8(5) of the CIRMP Rules concludes mid-2024. **Entities must have fully implemented the specified cybersecurity frameworks by this date.**

In addition to these overarching deadlines, the ECSO framework introduces specific reporting requirements for SoNS entities. For example:

- Entities must provide the Secretary of Home Affairs with a copy of their cyber incident response plan as soon as practicable after adopting it and whenever material changes are made to it.

- Following a cybersecurity exercise, entities must prepare an evaluation report and provide a copy to the Secretary within 30 days of the exercise's completion, unless otherwise directed.

- Vulnerability assessment reports must be submitted to the Secretary within 30 days of completion unless an extension is granted.

- System information reporting may be required on a periodic basis or in response to specific events, with timeframes specified in the relevant notice from the Secretary.

Critical infrastructure entities must know these compliance and reporting dates and engage early with the Cyber and Infrastructure Security Centre to clarify any specific requirements or deadlines applicable to their sector or asset. Proactive planning and resource allocation will be essential to ensure timely compliance with the SOCI Act reforms and the ECSO framework.

Mandatory Reporting

The Security of Critical Infrastructure Act 2018 (SOCI Act) requires responsible entities for critical infrastructure assets in Australia to report certain cybersecurity incidents mandatorily. This reporting obligation aims to give the government a comprehensive picture of emerging cyber threats and risks, enabling better partnerships with industries to mitigate serious cyberattacks. Reporting also allows the government to provide timely advice and support to entities during serious incidents:

- Could you please identify if a reportable cybersecurity incident has occurred, is occurring, or is imminent? This includes unauthorized access, and modification or impairment of computers, data, programs, or communications.

- Assess if the incident has had a "significant impact" (for critical incidents) or "relevant impact" (for other incidents) on the asset.

- A "significant impact" materially disrupts the availability of essential goods or services from the asset. Report critical incidents within 12 hours of becoming aware.

- A "relevant impact" is on the asset's availability, integrity, reliability, confidentiality, or information about/stored in it. Could you report other incidents within 72 hours of becoming aware?

- Reports are made to the Australian Cybersecurity Centre (ACSC). You are requested to provide details such as the impacted systems, incident description, estimated impact, and response steps taken.

- Some incidents, like scam emails or suspicious contacts, are generally only reportable if they lead to further infiltration and impact on the asset. When in doubt, err on the side of reporting.

- Reporting ensures the government can help protect all entities and the broader economy. Non-compliance may also lead to enforcement actions.

By instituting robust processes to identify and mandatorily report severe cyber incidents, entities will strengthen their cyber resilience while contributing to a collective national defense against the growing threat of cyberattacks on critical infrastructure. A proactive reporting partnership between industry and government is key to protecting Australia's economic and social well-being.

Where does AI Play a Role?

The impact of AI on the Security of Critical Infrastructure (SOCI), Enhanced Cybersecurity Obligations (ECSO), and Systems of National Significance (SoNS) is multifaceted and can be both positive and negative.

Positive impacts:

- **Improved threat detection:** AI-powered tools can analyze vast amounts of data from various sources, identifying potential cyber threats more quickly and accurately than traditional methods. This can help critical infrastructure entities detect and respond to incidents more effectively.

- **Enhanced situational awareness:** AI can help correlate and contextualize information from multiple sources, providing a more comprehensive understanding of the threat landscape and enabling better-informed decision-making.

- **Automated incident response:** AI-driven systems can automate certain aspects of incident response, such as isolating infected devices or updating firewall rules, reducing response times and minimizing the impact of cyber incidents on critical assets.

- **Predictive maintenance:** AI can analyze sensor data and historical performance records to predict when critical infrastructure components may fail, enabling proactive maintenance and reducing the risk of disruptions.

- **Compliance monitoring:** AI can help monitor and ensure compliance with ECSO requirements, such as identifying gaps in incident response plans or tracking the implementation of vulnerability remediation actions.

Negative impacts:

- **Increased attack surface:** Integrating AI systems into critical infrastructure may introduce new vulnerabilities and expand the attack surface, providing adversaries with new potential entry points.

- **AI-powered attacks:** Malicious actors can leverage AI to create more sophisticated and harder-to-detect attacks, such as adaptive malware or intelligent social engineering, making it more challenging for SoNS entities to defend against them.

- **Data poisoning:** Adversaries may attempt to manipulate the data used to train AI models, leading to incorrect decisions or actions that could compromise the security or resilience of critical assets.

- **Overreliance on AI:** Excessive dependence on AI systems may lead to complacency or a lack of human oversight, potentially allowing threats to go unnoticed or causing unintended consequences.

- **Ethical concerns:** The use of AI in critical infrastructure raises ethical questions around data privacy, algorithmic bias, and the potential for AI systems to make decisions that may have unintended societal impacts.

To maximize the benefits and mitigate the risks of AI in the context of SOCI, ECSO, and SoNS, critical infrastructure entities should:

- Adopt a balanced approach that leverages AI capabilities while maintaining human oversight and control.

- Implement robust security measures to protect AI systems and the data they process, which align with ECSO requirements.

- Regularly test and validate AI models to ensure accuracy, reliability, and alignment with organizational goals.

- To develop secure and effective AI solutions, foster collaboration between AI experts, cybersecurity professionals, and critical infrastructure operators.

- Stay informed about the latest developments in AI technology and its potential implications for critical infrastructure security.

By proactively addressing AI's challenges and opportunities, critical infrastructure entities can harness its power to enhance cyber resilience and better protect the nation's most vital assets.

Conclusion and Recommendations

The SOCI Act reforms and ECSO framework represent a substantial step-change in the security regulation of Australia's most critical infrastructure. The obligations will drive significant uplifts in the cyber resilience of crucial assets and the nation.

However, the ECSO imposes additional compliance and resourcing burdens for which SoNS entities must prepare. Entities should engage with government and leadership early to assess their status, understand requirements, and secure necessary funding and support.

Priority recommendations for SoNS entities include:

- Evaluate and refine cyber incident response plans against ECSO requirements, establish a regular testing and update cycle, and clearly understand reporting obligations under the SOCI Act.

- Design and deliver a multi-year cyber exercise program focused on likely, high-impact scenarios to maximize organizational learning and improvement.

- Continuously identify, prioritize, and remediate vulnerabilities across critical assets and systems through mature vulnerability management processes.

- Implement logging, monitoring, and reporting capabilities to fulfill system information-sharing obligations, aligning with broader situational awareness initiatives where possible.

- Drive executive understanding of ECSO implications and integrate uplifted resilience capabilities into strategic business continuity and risk management efforts.

- Establish processes to quickly identify reportable incidents, considering who in the organization would become aware of incidents and how they assess the level of impact.

- Assign clear internal reporting lines and responsibilities for submitting mandatory reports to ACSC within the required timeframes.

- During the first 12 months, focus on understanding the reporting thresholds. The government will prioritize education and guidance, with enforcement only for egregious breaches like failure to report critical incidents.

- Assess the specific impact of incidents on operations and services, referring to provided examples of "significant" versus. "relevant" impacts for different critical infrastructure sectors.

- When in doubt about an incident's reportability, contact the Cyber and Infrastructure Security Centre for advice. Lean towards reporting to enable government support and gain full visibility of the threat landscape.

While the ECSO introduces new demands, it provides a clear pathway for SoNS entities to elevate their cyber maturity. Forward-leaning, collaborative engagement with government partners will be key to efficient compliance and realizing the national security benefits envisioned by these critical reforms.

In a Nutshell

This chapter discussed the complex legal landscape around data privacy and law enforcement access to data. It compares the approaches of the United States, Europe, and Australia.

The U.S. CLOUD Act allows U.S. law enforcement agencies to access data stored by American tech companies regardless of where in the world that data is located. This creates conflicts with privacy laws in other jurisdictions like Australia and Europe. There are also concerns around a need for more transparency and notification if data is accessed under the CLOUD Act.

In contrast, Europe's GDPR gives individuals strong rights over their data, including consent, the right to deletion, and the right to be informed about data usage. The extraterritorial reach of the CLOUD Act could undermine these rights. There are jurisdictional conflicts between the GDPR, which aims to keep data in Europe, and the CLOUD Act, which allows U.S. access globally.

Australia faces its own complex balancing act between U.S. alliance, local privacy principles, and its own cybercrime laws. Australia's privacy principles are similar to GDPR, so there are comparable tensions with the CLOUD Act's global data access.

For companies, conflicting laws create compliance challenges and legal risks. Complying with U.S. requests under the CLOUD Act may breach EU or Australian privacy laws. This damages trust and reputation.

There are also sovereignty concerns around the U.S., potentially bypassing local legal processes. But the CLOUD Act also enables bilateral agreements to smooth cross-border data access.

Overall, conflicting national laws and approaches create a complex legal environment for data privacy and law enforcement access. Businesses must navigate carefully to balance compliance, trust, and reputation. Countries need to foster collaboration but also assert digital autonomy. The path ahead requires compromises between rights, security, transparency, and sovereignty.

Key Messages

- The U.S. CLOUD Act empowers U.S. law enforcement with global reach to access data held by American companies overseas, creating legal conflicts with other nations' privacy laws.

- Europe's GDPR provides individuals extensive control and rights over personal data that clash with the extraterritorial powers granted to the U.S. under the CLOUD Act.

- Australia must balance its privacy principles and local laws with the broad data access authorities afforded to its ally, the U.S., under the CLOUD Act.

- Corporations and government entities face compliance risks and legal jeopardy in complying with U.S. demands under the CLOUD Act, which may violate EU and other privacy laws, undermining trust.

- The CLOUD Act permits the U.S. to sidestep other countries' legal processes, challenging sovereignty and enabling streamlined law enforcement cooperation.

- Conflicting national laws spawn complex data privacy and access legal environments, requiring thoughtful navigation to balance compliance, trust, reputation, and public safety.

- Businesses must judiciously evaluate data jurisdiction and storage choices given disparate legal obligations across borders.

- Nations must champion collaboration on security while firmly asserting digital autonomy to strike compromises between individual rights, transparency, sovereignty, and law enforcement needs.

Five

International Conventions on Cybersecurity and eCommerce

Understanding the interplay between national law, public international law, and international conventions is vital for modern business management. The localized nature of national laws requires a tailored approach in each jurisdiction, while international laws and conventions create overarching frameworks that can shape cross-border operations. Staying informed and compliant with these legal landscapes is a fundamental responsibility for businesses, involving collaboration between legal teams, management, and other stakeholders.

International Conventions

International conventions on cybersecurity aim to promote cooperation and uniformity in combating cybercrime and securing cyberspace. I will start with a list of the key international conventions.

Budapest Convention on Cybercrime (2001)

Also known as: Council of Europe Convention on Cybercrime.

Key Areas: Includes provisions related to fraud, child pornography, copyright infringement, and network security.

Members: Open to all countries, though some nations have expressed reservations or have not ratified it.

Summary: The Budapest Convention on Cybercrime is a key international treaty that seeks to address rising computer and Internet-related crimes. It was enacted in 2001 to harmonize national cybercrime laws, improve investigative capabilities, and promote greater cooperation among nations to combat cybercrime effectively.

The Convention covers a range of cybercrime activities, including fraud, identity theft, child pornography, copyright infringement, and attacks against network security. It establishes cybercrimes as punishable criminal offenses and requires member countries to adopt legislative frameworks and tools for criminalizing these acts domestically.

Importantly, the Budapest Convention sets standards for international cooperation between signatories in investigating cybercrimes through mutual assistance and extradition arrangements. It also aims to build national capacity through procedures for accessing computer data and systems across borders in compliance with domestic legal requirements.

Though originally initiated by the Council of Europe, the Budapest Convention is open for signature by any country worldwide. Currently, 67 countries have signed and ratified the treaty, including the United States, United Kingdom, Japan, Canada, and South Africa. However, some countries like Russia, China, and India have expressed reservations and have not ratified it due to concerns over enabling foreign access to domestic data.

By promoting harmonization and cooperation, the Budapest Convention on Cybercrime represents an important foundation for developing a coordinated global response to curb cybercrime and ensure cybersecurity in our increasingly interconnected world. However, achieving broader agreement and adopting its provisions remains an ongoing challenge.

African Union Convention on Cybersecurity and Personal Data Protection (2014)

Objective: The African Union Convention on Cybersecurity and Personal Data Protection is a treaty that was adopted in 2014 to establish a harmonized legal framework for cybersecurity and data privacy across the African continent.

Key Areas: Focuses on electronic transactions, cybersecurity, and personal data protection.

Summary: Its core objective is to enable African nations to develop comprehensive national cybersecurity policies and regulatory mechanisms tailored to the African context. This includes facilitating electronic commerce, combating cybercrime, and protecting personal data.

Key areas covered by the convention include electronic transactions, cybersecurity, and personal data protection. For electronic transactions, it provides standards for issues like e-contracts, e-signatures, and e-evidence. Regarding cybersecurity, it mandates establishing bodies to respond to cyber threats and attacks.

Importantly, the convention emphasizes safeguarding personal data protection and privacy rights of citizens. It outlines conditions for lawful processing of personal data, including consent, lawful purpose, and notification. Individuals' rights to access and correct their personal data are also recognized.

By establishing shared norms and obligations, the African Union Convention aims to foster cooperation between

African states in tackling cybercrime and building cyber resilience while preserving constitutional rights and freedoms.

However, moving from convention to implementation remains a challenge, as only a handful of African Union member states have ratified it so far. However, if adopted more widely, it holds promise for creating a more trusted and harmonized cyber environment across Africa.

Shanghai Cooperation Organization Agreement on Cooperation in the Field of International Information Security (2009)

Objective: The Shanghai Cooperation Organization (SCO) Agreement on Cooperation in the Field of International Information Security is a treaty signed in 2009 between SCO member states, primarily Russia, China, and Central Asian countries.

Members: Primarily includes Russia, China, and other Central Asian countries.

Summary: Its core objective is to strengthen cooperation and coordination between these countries in the sphere of international information security. This covers threats to the political, economic, and social stability of SCO states posed by the use of information and communication technologies.

The agreement calls for joint efforts in developing international information security rules and standards. It aims to foster the sharing of best practices and technologies between national bodies responsible for information security.

It also seeks to prevent the dissemination of information damaging to the socio-political and socio-economic systems and spiritual and cultural environments of the SCO states. This reflects the authoritarian political systems of many of its members.

Additionally, the agreement advocates for limiting the presence of *information weapons*[15] in the information space of member states. This highlights the SCO's defensive posture against perceived information warfare by Western nations.

While critics argue the SCO framework may suppress Internet freedom, proponents believe it enables members to strengthen cyber sovereignty and counter cyber-enabled interference in their internal affairs.

By coordinating policies and rules governing national cyberspaces of member countries, the SCO agreement represents an attempt to shape a China and Russia-led model for cyber governance distinct from Western liberal norms.

---

[15] The term "information weapons" refers to tools, techniques, or technologies used to manipulate, disrupt, or destroy information systems or networks, essentially using information as a form of weapon in cyber warfare or information warfare. The term encapsulates a broad range of cyber tools that can be used for malicious purposes, including but not limited to malware, phishing schemes, and denial-of-service attacks.

Organization of American States (OAS) Inter-American Strategy to Combat Threats to Cybersecurity

Objective: The Inter-American Strategy to Combat Threats to Cybersecurity is a cooperative framework adopted by the Organization of American States (OAS) in 2004 to address the growing problem of cybersecurity threats across the Americas.

Key Areas: Focuses on legal measures, technical capabilities, organizational structures, capacity building, and international cooperation.

Summary: Its overarching objective is to establish a collaborative approach between OAS member states to prevent, confront, mitigate, and respond to cyber threats through legal and technical measures while respecting human rights and liberties.

The strategy identifies key areas for joint action, including establishing legal and regulatory frameworks, enhancing technical capabilities to protect critical infrastructure, developing organizational structures to respond to cyber incidents, building capacity through training and education, and fostering international cooperation.

Specific recommendations include adopting national cybersecurity policies and regulations in line with international standards, facilitating information sharing and crisis response coordination between national

CERTs/CSIRTs,[16] joint exercises to evaluate cyber incident readiness, and regional cooperation networks to combat cybercrime.

By articulating a shared doctrine that balances security with democratic principles, the OAS cybersecurity strategy aims to foster a collective approach to enhancing cyber resilience across the Americas.

However, its non-binding nature poses challenges in implementation. Still, the framework provides an important foundation for inter-state collaboration in strengthening cyber defenses.

ASEAN Cybersecurity Cooperation Strategy

Objective: The ASEAN Cybersecurity Cooperation Strategy is a policy framework adopted by the Association of Southeast Asian Nations (ASEAN) in 2016 to strengthen cybersecurity collaboration between its ten member states.

Key Areas: Focuses on harmonizing cybersecurity laws, sharing information, and building capabilities.

Summary: Its primary objective is to foster a resilient cyber environment in Southeast Asia through enhanced cooperation and coordination.

---

[16] A CERT (Computer Emergency Response Team) or CSIRT (Computer Security Incident Response Team) is a group tasked with responding to computer security incidents to prevent damage and manage the effects of security breaches.

Key focus areas include harmonizing national cybersecurity legal frameworks in line with global standards and best practices, facilitating real-time information sharing on threats and vulnerabilities between national cybersecurity centers, and developing cybersecurity capacity-building programs for law enforcement, government, and critical infrastructure operators.

Specific initiatives under the strategy include establishing baseline cybersecurity legal frameworks for ASEAN countries that lack comprehensive laws, setting up formal cooperation protocols between ASEAN CERTs/CSIRTS, developing early warning systems against cyberattacks, conducting joint cybersecurity exercises, and capacity building for law enforcement agencies to combat cybercrime.

By promoting greater harmonization of cybersecurity policies and response mechanisms between Southeast Asian countries, the ASEAN strategy aims to tackle the transboundary nature of cyber threats confronting the region.

However, disparities in national capabilities pose challenges for implementation. Still, the strategy signifies a growing recognition of the need for closer regional cooperation to enhance the region's collective cyber maturity and resilience.

European Union Cybersecurity Strategy and Directives

Objective: The European Union has developed a comprehensive cybersecurity strategy along with directives and regulations aimed at improving cyber resilience and response across the bloc.

Key Directives: Includes the Network and Information Security Directive, which sets a common level of network and information security within the EU.

Summary: The overarching EU Cybersecurity Strategy guides policy to strengthen cyber defense by enhancing cyber capabilities, cooperation, and partnerships. Key objectives include building EU-wide cyber incident response platforms, introducing common cybersecurity standards, and fostering research and industrial capabilities in cybersecurity technology.

Critical infrastructure protection is a top priority, addressed through the Network and Information Security (NIS) Directive. This directive establishes legal measures to boost the cybersecurity of essential services like energy, transport, banking, and digital infrastructure across the EU. It requires operators of critical services to implement risk management practices and report significant cyber incidents.

Additionally, the Cybersecurity Act creates a framework to provide cybersecurity certification for products and services to validate their compliance with security standards. The upcoming Data Act[17] also aims to enable secure data sharing between businesses and governments for public interest purposes.

Strategic partnerships are being forged with international organizations like NATO and key third countries to enhance cooperation on cyber deterrence, capacity building, and information sharing.

Together, these initiatives represent a comprehensive effort to harmonize cybersecurity policies, legal frameworks, and operational cooperation between EU member states and institutions to achieve strategic autonomy in cyberspace while upholding European values and human rights.

Global Cybersecurity Agenda (GCA) by the International Telecommunication Union (ITU)

Objective: The Global Cybersecurity Agenda (GCA) is a framework for international cooperation launched in 2007 by the International Telecommunication Union (ITU) to

---

[17] The provisional EU Data Act (June 2023) aims to foster a data-driven society in the EU by enhancing data access and usage rules. It grants consumers and companies more control over data generated by smart devices, emphasizing the function of collected data over the products themselves. The act also proposes measures to prevent unfair contractual terms in data-sharing agreements, safeguards trade secrets and intellectual property rights. It introduces mechanisms for dispute resolution and reasonable compensation for data access.

strengthen cybersecurity and build confidence in the information society.

Key Areas: Focuses on legal measures, technical and procedural measures, organizational structures, capacity building, and international cooperation.

Summary: Its overarching goal is to promote a strategic, cooperative approach to enhancing cybersecurity readiness and response at national, regional, and global levels.

Key focus areas include developing appropriate legal frameworks and technical standards, establishing organizational structures like CERTs for incident response, building capacity through training programs, and fostering partnerships between all stakeholders across government, private sector, academia, and civil society.

Specific initiatives pursued under the GCA include facilitating the adoption of national cybersecurity strategies, enabling real-time warning and response to cyber threats through mechanisms like AUTOSEC, promoting cybersecurity standards and best practices, creating training and certification programs, and marshaling resources and partnerships to build cybersecurity capacity globally.

As the leading United Nations agency on information and communication technologies, the ITU provides an inclusive platform to advance the GCA agenda through consensus-based international dialogue on norms and principles for cooperation in cyberspace.

By articulating a comprehensive vision spanning legal, technical, organizational, and capacity-building dimensions, the Global Cybersecurity Agenda serves as an important reference framework to guide multi-stakeholder efforts aimed at enhancing cybersecurity worldwide.

Hiroshima G7 AI Process Comprehensive Framework[18]

Objective: The Hiroshima AI Process (HAIP) Comprehensive Framework, endorsed by the G7 in 2023, establishes common ground for responsible development of advanced AI systems. It assesses how the HAIP's International Code of Conduct (HCOC) aligns with and can enhance interoperability between AI governance frameworks of G7 members. The G7 Member countries have expressed a unique role in shaping global AI governance, anchored in shared democratic values, human rights, and the rule of law. It identifies areas where the HCOC could be strengthened to provide more actionable guidance and serve as an international benchmark. Key considerations include coordinating terminology, robust risk management, harmonized stakeholder engagement, clear human rights safeguards, and exploring issues like government AI use, regulatory harmonization, and redress mechanisms. By addressing these areas, the HCOC can evolve into an impactful instrument for responsible AI

---

[18] [11] Habuka H., and Socol de la Osa D., May 2024, "Shaping Global AI Governance Enhancements and Next Steps for the G7 Hiroshima AI Process", Center for Strategic & International Studies.

development worldwide, ensuring AI benefits humanity while mitigating risks.

Key Areas:

1. The Hiroshima AI Process (HAIP) Comprehensive Framework, including the International Code of Conduct (HCOC), represents a significant milestone in international alignment on responsible AI development.

2. The HCOC aligns closely with existing AI governance trajectories in G7 nations, providing a foundation for interoperable frameworks and serving as a benchmark for the wider international community.

3. It is argued that the G7, as a group of leading democracies, is uniquely positioned to shape AI governance anchored in human rights, democratic values, and the rule of law through the HAIP.

4. To fully realize its potential, the HCOC requires further development to provide more specific, actionable guidance for practical implementation.

5. Key areas for enhancing the HCOC include coordinating terminology, robust risk management frameworks, harmonized stakeholder engagement standards, and concrete steps to uphold human rights principles.

6. The G7 could also leverage the HCOC to explore critical issues like government AI use, regulatory harmonization practices, fostering shared

responsibility in the AI ecosystem, and establishing redress mechanisms.

7. By strengthening the HCOC, the G7 can develop it into a robust global reference point for responsible AI development, ensuring AI benefits all while mitigating risks and upholding core values.

8. International alignment through an enhanced HCOC can drive cohesive AI governance practices worldwide, facilitating innovation while safeguarding societal interests.

Summary: The Hiroshima AI Process (HAIP) Comprehensive Framework, endorsed by the G7 in 2023, marks a pivotal moment in the global governance of artificial intelligence (AI). Central to this framework is the Hiroshima Process International Code of Conduct (HCOC), which establishes guidelines for the responsible development and deployment of advanced AI systems. As the world grapples with the rapid advancement of AI technologies, the HCOC emerges as a beacon, offering direction and principles to ensure AI progress aligns with fundamental human values.

The significance of the HAIP and HCOC cannot be overstated. As a collaborative effort by the world's leading democracies, the G7 nations, this framework carries substantial weight and influence. It represents a shared commitment to steering AI development in a direction that upholds human rights, democratic principles, and the rule of law. By setting this course, the G7 demonstrates leadership and vision, recognizing that the power of AI must be harnessed responsibly for the benefit of all humanity.

The HCOC, as it stands, closely aligns with the existing AI strategies and regulations taking shape within G7 countries. This alignment is crucial, as it lays the groundwork for interoperability – the ability for different nations' AI governance frameworks to work together seamlessly. Interoperability is essential in our interconnected world, where AI systems and their impacts transcend borders. By providing a common reference point, the HCOC facilitates coordination and consistency across jurisdictions. However, while the HCOC establishes important principles, it currently lacks the specificity needed to provide detailed, practical guidance for implementation. To fully realize its potential as a global benchmark, the HCOC must evolve and expand. This evolution should focus on several key areas:

First, the HCOC should work towards a shared understanding of critical AI terminology. A common language is essential for clear communication and consistent interpretation of AI governance principles across borders. Second, the HCOC should provide comprehensive guidance on risk management. This includes frameworks for identifying and mitigating potential harms throughout the AI lifecycle, from development to deployment and ongoing monitoring. Third, the HCOC should promote harmonized standards for stakeholder engagement and transparency. Clear, consistent practices for involving and informing all parties impacted by AI systems are crucial for fostering public trust. Fourth, the HCOC must offer concrete, actionable measures to safeguard human rights and uphold democratic values in the context of AI. This goes beyond broad principles to provide specific steps for protecting privacy, preventing discrimination, and ensuring accountability.

Finally, the G7 should leverage the HCOC as a platform to explore critical emerging issues in AI governance. This includes developing guidelines for government use of AI, establishing best practices for regulatory coordination, defining roles and responsibilities across the AI ecosystem, and creating mechanisms for redress when AI systems cause harm.

By addressing these areas, the G7 can shape the HCOC into a robust, comprehensive instrument for responsible AI governance. A strengthened HCOC will serve not only the G7 but the international community as a whole. It will provide a solid foundation upon which nations can build their own AI strategies, confident that they are aligned with global best practices.

According to the authors and signatories of the Hiroshima Protocol the path forward is clear. By investing in the development of the HCOC, the G7 can lead the way towards a future where AI is a force for good, a tool that enhances our lives while respecting our fundamental values. The HAIP Comprehensive Framework and the HCOC represent the first steps on this journey. With commitment, collaboration, and a shared vision, we can ensure that the transformative power of AI benefits all of humanity. The G7 has the opportunity and the responsibility to guide this process, and the world is watching.

Common Themes Amongst International Conventions

These conventions and agreements reflect a growing global concern about cybersecurity and a recognition that international cooperation is crucial to combating cyber threats. Understanding the legal obligations under these frameworks is essential for businesses operating internationally, as non-compliance can lead to legal risks and reputational damage. There are common themes and shared objectives amongst each of these conventions:

- **Harmonizing Laws and Standards:** There is a shared emphasis on harmonizing national cybersecurity laws, regulations, and technical standards between countries through international conventions.

- **International Cooperation:** Enhancing international cooperation on cybersecurity through information sharing, joint investigations, and cross-border coordination is a consistent priority.

- **Capacity Building:** Developing national cyber capabilities through organizational structures, training programs, and public-private partnerships is a recurring theme.

- **Critical Infrastructure Protection:** Safeguarding critical infrastructure like energy, transportation, and digital systems from cyber threats is a high priority across the conventions.

- **Balancing Security Rights and Liberties:** Finding an equilibrium between improving cybersecurity and preserving rights like privacy and the free flow of information is an acknowledged challenge.

- **Multi-stakeholder Approach:** Involving all stakeholders, including governments, private sector, academia, and civil society, in cyber governance is a widely embraced principle.

- **Regional Frameworks:** Cybersecurity conventions organized around regional structures and priorities act as stepping stones toward global norms.

- **Challenges in Adoption:** Moving from agreement to concrete adoption and implementation of conventions remains an uphill task.

While differing in specifics, these conventions reveal an emerging consensus on a cooperative, capacity-building approach grounded in the rule of law to address the borderless challenge of cybersecurity.

In a Nutshell

International conventions and regional accords on cybersecurity establish crucial frameworks for cooperation between nation-states to combat cybercrime and build cyber resilience. These agreements aim to harmonize national laws, facilitate information sharing, develop response capabilities, and forge partnerships across borders to tackle the borderless challenge of cyber threats.

The Budapest Convention on Cybercrime, with over 60 signatories, is a landmark treaty that obligates countries to criminalize cyber offenses domestically and enables joint investigations through mutual legal assistance. Regional accords like the African Union Convention, Shanghai Cooperation Organization Agreement, and OAS Strategy articulate tailored approaches aligned with the priorities of member states. The ASEAN and EU cybersecurity strategies focus on strengthening collaboration within their respective blocs.

While differing in specifics, these conventions consistently emphasize the need to balance security imperatives with rights such as privacy and freedom of expression. They advocate capacity building through shared policies, technical standards, and organizational structures. Safeguarding critical infrastructure is a persistent priority.

A multi-stakeholder model involving governments, businesses, academia, and civil society is widely endorsed. Regional cooperation is seen as a pathway toward building international norms. However, adopting and implementing conventions' provisions remain an ongoing challenge.

Understanding obligations under pertinent cybersecurity conventions is imperative for businesses, as non-compliance risks legal jeopardy and reputation damage. Management must be aware of relevant frameworks and ensure operations align with requirements.

As cyber threats exploit interconnections between nations, international conventions will grow in importance for the governance of cyberspace. While negotiating common ground is complex, these accords represent a maturing recognition that cybersecurity demands cooperation, not just within domestic domains but globally.

Key Messages

- **Importance of Conventions:** International conventions on cybersecurity are crucial for fostering cooperation among nations to combat cyber threats and ensure cyber resilience.

- **Localized Laws, International Standards:** The localized nature of national laws requires businesses to tailor their approach to each jurisdiction, while international conventions provide overarching frameworks that guide cross-border operations.

- **Complex Interplay:** The interplay between national laws, international conventions, and public international law creates a complex landscape that demands collaboration between legal teams, management, and stakeholders.

- **Shared Objectives:** Conventions share common objectives, such as harmonizing laws and standards, promoting international cooperation, building capacity, protecting critical infrastructure, and balancing security with individual rights.

- **Multi-Stakeholder Approach:** A multi-stakeholder model involving governments, businesses, academia, and civil society is endorsed, recognizing that cybersecurity is a collective responsibility.

- **Challenges in Adoption:** Despite their importance, moving from convention agreement to implementation remains a challenge, requiring sustained efforts.

- **Business Compliance:** Businesses must understand and comply with these frameworks to avoid legal repercussions and reputational damage.

- **Global Cyber Landscape:** With cyber threats transcending borders, these conventions will continue to shape the global response to cybersecurity challenges.

- **Ongoing Relevance:** The conventions' relevance highlights the need for businesses to navigate a complex regulatory environment while ensuring the security of their digital operations.

- **Collective Responsibility:** These agreements reflect a maturing recognition that cybersecurity demands cooperation at a global scale, emphasizing the need for collaboration among nations and stakeholders.

Six

Managing Cyber Risk

> "Cyber-security incidents have been estimated to cost Australian businesses up to $29 billion per year and cybercrime affected almost one in three Australian adults in 2018. At the same time, serious cyber incidents like WannaCry, Cloud Hopper, and the intrusion into Australia's parliamentary networks illustrate the threat to our economy, democracy, and way of life."
>
> Excerpt from "Australia's 2020 Cybersecurity Strategy"

In the realm of cybersecurity, risk assessment and analysis stand as integral components of a comprehensive defense strategy. This chapter delves into the multifaceted nature of these concepts, highlighting the complexity and interconnectedness of the various stages involved in identifying, understanding, and mitigating cyber risks.

199

Understanding Risk

The chapter begins by demystifying the concept of risk within the context of information and information systems. It discusses the theoretical underpinnings of risk, its various manifestations, and how it acts as a catalyst that can influence the overall security posture. One can lay the groundwork for targeted, effective risk management strategies by defining and categorizing risks.

This section provides a broad exploration of risk assessment methodologies. It explains how to systematically identify, evaluate, and prioritize risks, leading to informed decision-making. By employing qualitative and quantitative techniques, organizations can create a robust framework that accounts for threats, vulnerabilities, and potential impacts. This process allows for a tailored approach that aligns with the unique requirements, goals, and constraints of a specific environment.

Stages of an Attack

We will explore the intricate stages of a cyberattack. Starting from the initial reconnaissance phase to the final actions on objectives, it outlines how attackers plan, execute, and capitalize on vulnerabilities. The analysis includes a detailed look at tactics, techniques, and procedures, shedding light on how threat actors maneuver through a system. Understanding these stages is paramount for developing both preventive and reactive defenses.

Defense or Offence?

Within the spectrum of defense, there are various strategies ranging from passive to offensive measures. This part of the chapter dissects these strategies, elaborating on how they can help bolster security. Passive defenses may include measures like firewalls and intrusion detection systems, while offensive strategies might involve active threat-hunting and counter-attack mechanisms. The balance between these defensive postures requires careful consideration and alignment with legal, ethical, and organizational guidelines.

In synthesizing these core components, this chapter provides a holistic perspective on cybersecurity risk assessment and analysis. It offers both theoretical insights and practical guidance, serving as a resource for professionals seeking to fortify their cyber defenses. The understanding gleaned from this chapter not only facilitates the implementation of robust security measures but fosters a culture of continuous improvement, adaptability, and resilience. It equips readers with the knowledge and tools needed to navigate the ever-evolving cyber landscape, ensuring preparedness in the face of constant change.

Understanding Risk

In the challenging landscape of today's interconnected business world, three concepts stand out as fundamental: risk, threat, and vulnerability. They interact in complex ways, shaping the contours of our security environment.

Risk is the probability that a vulnerability will be exploited, leading to potential loss or damage. It's the alarming blend of the chance of something harmful happening and the aftermath if it does occur.

A **Threat**, on the other hand, is the dark shadow of someone or something that might exploit a vulnerability, whether intentionally or accidentally, turning a latent risk into a real one.

Vulnerability is the underlying weakness that might be exploited, the chink in the armor that allows the threat to manifest as risk.

The art of information risk management builds on these concepts. It's a disciplined, systematic approach to identifying, evaluating, and controlling risks to keep them within acceptable bounds. But what does this mean in practice? Consider the many facets of modern organizational life that can be affected, ranging from physical damage, such as fire or water, to human intervention, equipment malfunction, data breaches, and intentional or unintentional information loss. Assessment and identification of these areas using both qualitative and quantitative methodologies are vital yet intricate parts of effective risk management.

Cybersecurity, though just one of many types of risk an organization must address, assumes particular importance in our increasingly digital age. With organizational networks everywhere and a significant dependency on the Internet, cybersecurity has become a focal point in information risk management.

We see a multifaceted, dynamic process when we delve into security management within this context. An effective information security risk management policy must be integral to the broader risk management strategy. It starts with a rigorous assessment of risks, determining what needs protection. Constant monitoring and evaluation are required to ensure that the systems and practices in place are effective. But it doesn't stop there–every individual within the organization must be aware of the potential risks and trained to act appropriately. Management must also allocate adequate resources, including funds, guided by a risk acceptance level defined by senior leadership.

Compliance, metrics, and performance criteria are essential elements that ensure alignment with legal requirements and continual optimization. Adaptation and integration play crucial roles as well. With a constantly changing landscape, the ability to identify and address new risks is vital. The integration of risk management with other organizational processes is a key aspect of preventing the unintentional introduction of new vulnerabilities.

In conclusion, in a world where 100% security is an unattainable dream, information risk management doesn't seek to eliminate every threat. Instead, its role is to systematically reduce them to levels that the organization deems acceptable. It's an ongoing, cyclical process that calls for a coordinated and sophisticated approach from the entire organization. Managing risk is a matter of balance, neither complacent nor paranoid, always vigilant, flexible, and responsive. The wisdom in managing risk is in recognizing this delicate balance and acting with purpose and insight. It's not just a matter of business—it's a matter of organizational integrity and resilience.

The concept of OODA (Observe, Orient, Decide, Act) has been a critical part of strategic thinking, particularly in military contexts. Here's a short case study that focuses on the application of the OODA Loop within the U.S. Air Force.

Case Study: The U.S. Air Force and the OODA Loop

The OODA Loop was introduced by Air Force Colonel John Boyd, and it has had a profound impact on military strategy, particularly within the U.S. Air Force. The concept is designed to provide a framework for decision-making that is both iterative and adaptive. OODA follows the PDCA[19] Model of W. Edwards Deming, a core component of Quality Management and is applied consistently in Agile project management methodologies.

---

[19] Plan Do Check Act.

This case study explores the origin, implementation, and effects of the OODA Loop within the U.S. Air Force.

The Origin of the Concept

John Boyd, a fighter pilot and military strategist, developed the concept of the OODA Loop. It began as an analysis of air combat but later evolved into a broad decision-making process. Boyd realized that success in a rapidly changing environment required continuous assessment and adaptation. The four stages of the OODA Loop (Observe, Orient, Decide, Act) provided a way to understand this dynamic cycle.

Application within the U.S. Air Force

The U.S. Air Force adopted the OODA Loop as a core principle for tactical training and air combat scenarios. Pilots were trained to observe their surroundings, orient themselves to the situation, decide on the best course of action, and then act swiftly. By cycling through these stages rapidly and repeatedly, they could outmaneuver opponents.

Beyond combat, the Air Force integrated the OODA Loop into strategic planning and operational methodologies. It was used to enhance situational awareness and facilitate rapid decision-making in various aspects of military operations, from logistics to intelligence analysis.

Impact on the U.S. Air Force

The OODA Loop provided the U.S. Air Force with a framework to increase agility and responsiveness. It allowed for quick adaptation to changes on the battlefield, enabling superior positioning and action.

By emphasizing iterative learning and continuous improvement, the OODA Loop helped build a culture within the Air Force that values adaptability and resilience. It fostered a mindset that encourages continuous observation and learning, leading to informed decisions.

Influence on Other Domains

The success of the OODA Loop in the Air Force led to its adoption in other military branches and even civilian sectors, where it has been used to enhance decision-making in complex, rapidly changing environments.

Adopting the OODA Loop by the U.S. Air Force has proved to be a transformational concept. It encapsulated a process of continuous, adaptive decision-making crucial in modern warfare's volatile environment. The legacy of John Boyd's idea continues to resonate, not only within the Air Force but across various domains where decision-making is central. The U.S. Air Force's application of the OODA Loop illustrates the timeless nature of the principle, demonstrating that agility, adaptability, and continuous learning are fundamental to success in an ever-changing world.

Risk Assessment and Analysis

In a world where digital presence is ever-growing, understanding the landscape of risk in cybersecurity is of utmost importance. As we embark on this chapter, we find ourselves on a journey that will take us through the complex terrains of risk analysis, cyberattacks, and defense.

In the intricate web of business management, the twin concepts of risk assessment and risk analysis often surface, intertwined yet distinct, like the double helix of a DNA molecule. At first glance, they may seem synonymous, but upon closer examination, their unique roles and contributions to risk management become evident.

Picture a panoramic view of a sprawling city, complete with towering skyscrapers, bustling streets, and a kaleidoscope of activities. This panoramic view is akin to risk assessment—a broad, overarching process that seeks to identify, analyze, evaluate, and ultimately manage risks. It's like a seasoned cartographer drawing up a complex map, detailing every lane and pathway, assessing roadblocks, and noting potential safe havens. Risk assessment is holistic—it assembles a big picture view of all potential risks, weighing their priorities and outlining a treatment plan. This sweeping survey integrates various data points, from risk audits and surveys to business impact analyses.

Now, zero in on a single building within that sprawling city. Look closely at its structure, the quality of materials used, and the environmental risks surrounding it. This focused analysis is what we call risk analysis. It's the architect at work, deep in concentration, calculating the stress and strain different materials can bear, analyzing seismic data, and determining the building's vulnerability to specific risks. Risk analysis is more focused, zooming in on the particulars, on the "how" and "why" of each risk. It employs specialized tools, like threat intelligence and vulnerability scans, to quantify and articulate factors such as the likelihood of a risk occurring and its potential impact.

Risk assessment uses the results of this intensive risk analysis as foundational pillars upon which to construct treatment plans. It makes calculated decisions on mitigating, accepting, transferring, or avoiding risks based on the rich, nuanced insights provided by risk analysis. The output of a risk assessment is often a dynamic risk register that lists risks, rates them, and specifies a treatment strategy for each, whereas the output of risk analysis is more granular, providing specific metrics like likelihood and impact levels.

To keep this metaphorical city thriving and resilient, risk assessment doesn't just lay dormant after its initial implementation. Instead, it revisits its panoramic view periodically, scanning for changes in the city's landscape, perhaps due to new construction or climate change. Risk analysis, in contrast, is often more continual, acting as the city's vigilant watchman, constantly monitoring data feeds for new emerging threats or vulnerabilities.

Different teams with different skills and experiences often perform this intricate dance between risk assessment and risk analysis. Risk assessment usually calls upon a team of risk managers, auditors, and subject matter experts (logistics, banking, etc.) to piece together its panoramic view. On the other hand, risk analysis often demands specialized expertise in statistical and financial modeling—

professionals who can delve deep into the nitty-gritty of each potential risk.

While risk assessment paints the grand tapestry of risks in bold strokes, risk analysis fills in the critical details with fine brushwork. One lays out the terrain, and the other charts the course, and it's through their collaborative synergy that organizations achieve a nuanced, comprehensive approach to risk management.

Digging a little deeper

As we delve further into the landscape of risk, we encounter four dimensions:

- threat,
- loss (impact),
- controls, and
- assets

each treated subtly differently by various standards and methodologies.

Risk analysis is a vital tool that enables organizations to uncover vulnerabilities, assess uncertainties, and strategically mitigate risks.

We will continue this chapter by exploring the foundations of risk analysis, which involves identifying key assets, evaluating their value, pinpointing threats, gauging controls, and estimating potential impacts. Precise methodologies like FAIR (Factor Analysis of Information Risk) help organizations move beyond subjective risk ratings to conduct more quantifiable analyses. Standards such as ISO 27001 offer frameworks to guide the risk analysis process.

We need to include four key landscapes in the risk analysis process–threats, loss/impacts, controls, and assets. We will examine each of these in more detail (but not too much), looking at critical considerations such as threat frequency, control effectiveness, potential damage scenarios, and asset valuations. A diverse risk analysis team is crucial to represent different perspectives across these landscapes.

Figure 2: Threat Landscape.

Threat Landscape

The threat landscape encompasses the external risks that can adversely affect an organization's assets and operations. Threat analysis examines factors like threat actors, their capabilities, intent, and targeting. We consider both natural threats like floods and human-caused threats like cyberattacks. Statistical modeling tools determine threat frequencies, while threat intelligence provides insights into emerging hazards. Understanding the threat landscape is crucial for estimating the likelihood of specific threat scenarios materializing. This landscape continuously evolves, necessitating frequent re-evaluation of probabilities and potential business impacts.

Loss (Impact) Landscape

The loss or impact landscape deals with the harm that could result from threat events. It encompasses all categories of adverse impacts like financial losses, operational disruptions, reputational damages, and regulatory non-compliance. Impact assessment utilizes techniques like incident scenarios, financial modeling, and business impact analysis to estimate potential consequences under different threat situations. Both quantitative impacts, like monetary losses, and qualitative impacts, like loss of public trust, are examined. This understanding of probable consequences across varied risk categories and business areas enables focused mitigation efforts and continuity planning.

Controls Landscape

The controls landscape encompasses the policies, procedures, technologies, and controls implemented to reduce risks. It involves identifying existing controls through surveys and audits, and evaluating their effectiveness against specific threats. Metrics like the percentage of vulnerable systems patched or users trained indicate control strength. New planned controls are also assessed for potential risk reduction. This landscape determines control gaps and opportunities for improvement. It provides data to adjust probabilities in light of control strengths and weaknesses.

Assets Landscape

The assets landscape covers the resources that both require protection from threats, but also are the assets used by your organization to provide you with protection. It includes information on asset types, values, business criticality, dependencies, and existing vulnerabilities. Asset valuation utilizes methods like replacement costs, revenue contribution, and proprietary value. Detailed asset profiles (think about your critical infrastructure components) enable focused safeguards, controls, and risk reduction efforts. They also feed into potential loss forecasts by clarifying the impact of asset damage or loss. This landscape provides the foundation for risk management.

Risk Assessment and Analysis Tools

At its core, effective risk analysis is as fundamental to an organization as a keel is to a ship. It steadies the course, providing essential balance and direction. One can't just dive headlong into this—you must first recognize what you're defending—the organizational assets that provide you with the capability of conducting business safely. Think of these assets like pieces on a chessboard, each with its role, vulnerabilities, and value. Now, knowing your assets allows you to spot potential threats like those ominous storm clouds looming on your business horizon.

But we don't stop there. We also assess the moat and walls we've built around our castle—these are your existing controls and safeguards. And we ask, are they sturdy enough to repel an invading army? We will use methodologies like FAIR (Factor Analysis of Information Risk), the sharp analytical lens that transforms fuzzy estimations into quantifiable metrics. It's akin to replacing a hand-drawn sketch with a high-resolution photograph—the details become strikingly clear, offering a more nuanced understanding that transcends mere gut feelings or qualitative judgments.

Imagine trying to explain the Sistine Chapel ceiling to someone who's never seen it. Words can do it little justice, but a picture? A single glance can convey a wealth of information. This is the role visual tools like risk heat maps play. They distill convoluted data into a format easily digestible by everyone from board members to frontline staff. A heat map can turn abstract risks into concrete visuals, allowing you to prioritize and link these risks back to the broader strategic aims of your organization. You expertly bring together your organization's diverse components into harmonious alignment, like an inspirational conductor uniting an orchestra. It's as if you don infrared goggles to illuminate once-invisible aspects in the shadow—the landscape appears hazy but newly visible, opening up possibilities.

Heat Maps facilitate risk prioritization and communication across the organization. However, overreliance on historical data is cautioned against, especially when predicting rare events. Here, expert analysis is vital to account for continuously evolving threats.

Risk heat maps are invaluable visualization tools in the risk analysis process. They help to organize and succinctly communicate the key risks that might impact a company. A heat map can range from simple (showing only qualitative risks) to complex (including both qualitative and quantitative risks). Figure 3 shows an example of a color-coded heat map.

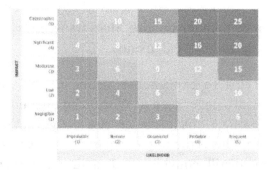

Figure 3: Color-coded heat map (https://www.techtarget.com)

Additional elements like risk registers, ROI estimations, and business impact analysis are part of an integrated risk management framework. Bureaucratic approaches are warned against, emphasizing that flexibility and adaptability are key. Approximations are sometimes necessary for complex costs, guided by ethical transparency regarding uncertainties and limitations.

But let's not forget — the map is not the territory. While historical data and statistical methods give us a strong foundation, they can't predict black swan events—those rare, unprecedented occurrences that defy our best models. This is where seasoned expertise earns its weight in gold. It compensates for the inherent blind spots in data, providing the nuance needed to navigate uncharted waters.

Let's add another layer to our tapestry: key concepts like risk registers, ROI analysis, and business impact evaluations. Consider these the compass, sextant, and maps of your exploratory expedition. They ensure that you're not only identifying risks but are actively planning out routes to circumnavigate or tackle them head-on, always in alignment with your ultimate treasure—your organizational objectives.

Now, beware of the siren call of bureaucracy. Paper-pushing, box-ticking exercises masquerading as risk assessments can be as dangerous as sailing into a storm unprepared. Flexibility and adaptability are your allies, allowing you to recalibrate your compass as the winds change. Ethical considerations, especially when estimating ambiguous costs, are not just mere footnotes but core chapters in your risk management epic. Full transparency here is not a luxury–it's a necessity.

So, in the grand finale of our intellectual symphony, we understand that robust risk analysis is not a solo act—it's a grand ensemble performance. It's a dynamic equilibrium between hard, quantifiable data and the softer yet invaluable qualitative insights. This duality serves as your North Star, guiding you through the treacherous, ever-changing seas of the modern business landscape.

By making risk analysis a core competency, organizations don't just survive—they can thrive, gaining new ground and responding faster to changing circumstances. They weather storms, avoid icebergs, and discover new lands—always with an eye on that ultimate treasure: a secure, prosperous future.

To summarize:

- Risk analysis involves asset valuation, threat identification, control analysis, and impact assessment. It helps organizations understand uncertainties and vulnerabilities.

- Precise methodologies like FAIR (Factor Analysis of Information Risk) enable more meaningful risk analysis versus subjective ratings.

- Key elements in risk analysis include identifying assets, threats, controls, impacts, and measuring risk factors. Standards like ISO 27001 provide a framework.

- Four key sources of risk information are threats, loss/impacts, controls, and assets. Understanding the landscape of each is crucial.

- Threat analysis involves assessing threat frequency and capability to harm assets. Threats must be clearly classified.

- Control analysis examines existing and planned controls, and estimates their effectiveness in reducing vulnerabilities.

- Impact analysis uses techniques like scenarios to estimate potential damage from information security incidents.

- Risk analysis teams should have diverse expertise, representing various organizational functions and roles.

- Risk heat maps visually display risks by likelihood and impact. They help prioritize responses and enhance communication.

- Statistics are indispensable in risk management but have limitations in predicting rare events due to insufficient data.

- Assessing information security involves expert judgment to address continuously evolving threats.

- Risk registers catalog risks and mitigation strategies. They connect to ROI analysis for economic rationality.

- Bureaucratic risk assessment can lead to rigid, superficial analysis and delayed responses. Balance with flexibility is key.

- Business impact analysis examines the financial, reputational, and compliance impacts of incidents. It informs risk strategies.

- Estimating complex business costs involves approximations and methodologies to address multivariate, indirect costs.

- Risk management requires comprehensive, thoughtful, non-bureaucratic practices tailored to the organization.

Stages of an Attack

In today's rapidly advancing digital world, the threat of cyberattacks is more present than ever. Just as a carefully planned physical heist might take place in a bank or art gallery, cybercriminals orchestrate virtual attacks to breach security measures, steal valuable information, and even manipulate systems. Understanding these threats requires insight into the stages of a cyberattack, a process that can be compared to a meticulously planned criminal endeavor.

"The Stages of an Attack" is a model that breaks down the complex process of a cyberattack into more manageable phases. It provides a structured framework to understand how an attack unfolds, from the initial planning and reconnaissance to the final execution and possible aftermath.

Preparation

Before a cyberattack, criminals conduct detailed planning and analysis, similar to a team of thieves casing a bank. This includes gathering information about the target, understanding its weaknesses, and selecting the best tools for the job. They might explore various security measures, look for open doors in the system, and even conduct trial runs. This stage is about knowing the target inside out and crafting the most effective plan of attack.

Intrusion

Next, they breach the defenses, akin to breaking into the vault. This involves exploiting vulnerabilities in the system, such as weak passwords, outdated software, or even manipulating employees through methods like phishing. The criminals work stealthily, making sure not to alert security mechanisms, much like burglars avoiding security cameras and alarms.

Active Breach

Once inside, they actively exploit what they've accessed. This stage sees the thieves in action, stealing, altering, or destroying valuable information. They might sell personal data on the dark web or use insider knowledge to manipulate stock prices. The possibilities are vast and damaging.

Understanding these stages–preparation, intrusion, and active breach– is not merely an academic exercise–it's a crucial part of defending against cyber threats. By recognizing the steps that attackers take, organizations can better anticipate potential risks, implement appropriate defenses, and respond effectively if an attack occurs.

The model of *"The Stages of an Attack"* offers a lens through which managers, even without technical expertise, can grasp the intricate dynamics of cybersecurity. It helps in translating the often abstract world of cyber threats into concrete terms, drawing parallels with familiar real-world scenarios. This understanding forms the foundation for a robust and responsive cybersecurity strategy, helping to safeguard an organization in an environment where threats constantly evolve.

Case Study: WannaCry Ransomware Virus

In May 2017, the digital landscape was struck with a virulent threat known as the WannaCry ransomware attack. Targeting Windows-based PCs across 156 countries, it encrypted data on 200,000 machines, demanding ransom payments. Microsoft's preemptive security patch was ignored by many, leaving them susceptible to this cyber onslaught.

County Durham and Darlington NHS Foundation Trust (CDDFT) within the British healthcare system experienced the indirect consequences of this attack. Various segments of the healthcare system were affected, each responding with measures to mitigate the damage:

Here's an expanded narrative on the impact of the WannaCry ransomware attack on the Ambulance Service within County Durham and Darlington NHS Foundation Trust (CDDFT):

In the tumultuous wake of the WannaCry ransomware attack, various sectors of the healthcare industry were affected, each grappling with unique challenges. Among them, the Ambulance Service within CDDFT faced an urgent situation.

How it Affected the Ambulance Service

The primary blow to the Ambulance Service was the disruption to the handover process. As the ransomware swept through the digital infrastructure, encrypting data, the electronic screens used to facilitate ambulance handover were rendered inoperative.

However, this didn't spell defeat for the Ambulance Service. Quick thinking led to a reversion to more primitive yet effective means of communication. Pre-alerts, which are critical information about incoming emergencies, continued to be communicated via landlines. Ambulances arrived without digital warning, but vital information about patients, known as 'pins,' was transmitted via airwaves.

This improvised solution bridged the gap left by the digital failure, ensuring that the front-line responders remained operational and that patient care was not compromised.

The ransomware also paralyzed the Patient Transport Service booking portal. This digital portal, vital for scheduling patient transport, was knocked offline, threatening to cause delays and confusion.

Once again, the Ambulance Service proved its adaptability. Invoking the Business Continuity Plan (BCP), bookings were made via telephone. This manual process, though less efficient, allowed the service to continue functioning and maintain its commitment to patient care.

The experience served as a stark reminder of the vulnerabilities inherent in relying on digital systems. It led to a robust review and updating of the CDDFT Business Continuity Plan. The new plan includes detailed measures to ensure continued communication in the event of future cyber threats, with particular attention to integrating landline, mobile, and airwave communications.

The Ambulance Service's response to the WannaCry attack is a case study of resilience and ingenuity. In the face of unexpected and severe digital disruption, the service maintained its vital functions through adaptive thinking and resourceful use of alternative communication methods.

Moreover, the incident became a catalyst for introspection and learning. Lessons were derived, plans were reevaluated, and strategies were enhanced. It highlighted the importance of having versatile and comprehensive contingency plans in place, reinforcing that technology is a tool, not a crutch, and that human resourcefulness and adaptability remain paramount in crisis management.

The tale of the Ambulance Service within CDDFT during the WannaCry ransomware attack stands as a testament to the agility, dedication, and foresight that define effective emergency response in our interconnected age. It illustrates how, even in an era of advanced technology, fundamental human traits like resilience and adaptability continue to be the linchpin of effective service delivery.

How it Affected Tertiary Medical Centers

The WannaCry ransomware attack had profound effects on various sectors of the healthcare industry, and the tertiary centers within County Durham and Darlington NHS Foundation Trust (CDDFT) were no exception. These centers, responsible for specialized consultative health care, found themselves caught in a web of technological disruption. Here's an in-depth look at how they were affected:

Disruption in Transferring CT/MR Scans

Tertiary centers often serve as hubs for advanced diagnostic imaging, such as CT and MRI scans. When the WannaCry ransomware encrypted the systems, the digital channels used to transfer these vital images were blocked. The digital pathways that usually transported critical medical information with speed and accuracy were effectively severed.

In the face of this obstruction, the tertiary centers displayed both innovation and resolve. They resorted to transferring the images onto DVDs and sending them via taxi. Though less efficient than the digital methods, this approach ensured that vital diagnostic information reached the necessary medical professionals, albeit at a slower pace.

Impact on Chemo Care

The ransomware attack's reach extended into the very heart of cancer treatment. Chemo Care, the system responsible for managing and transferring chemotherapy orders to providers, was cut off. The digitized lifeline that linked patients to potentially life-saving treatments was abruptly snapped.

Yet, resilience prevailed. Tertiary centers reverted to paper and faxed the chemo orders, demonstrating adaptability in the face of an unprecedented digital crisis. While less efficient and more time-consuming, this manual method kept the critical flow of chemotherapy treatment moving, reaffirming the commitment to patient care.

Lessons and Future Planning

The impact of the WannaCry attack was not lost on the tertiary centers. It prompted reflection, learning, and action. The lessons led to purchasing secondary DVDs, fortifying the alternative image transfer method. A specific Business Continuity Plan (BCP) for Chemo Care was created, detailing the actions to be taken in the event of another cyberattack.

This was not merely a reactive step but a proactive measure to ensure that future threats would meet with a fortified response.

The experience of the tertiary centers within CDDFT during the WannaCry ransomware attack is a vivid illustration of the complexities and vulnerabilities of healthcare in a digital age. It's also a powerful testament to the adaptability, innovation, and unwavering commitment to patient care that characterized the response.

In the face of sudden and unprecedented disruption, the tertiary centers found ways to keep essential services running. They also took the lessons to heart, transforming a crisis into an opportunity for growth and future preparedness.

Their story underscores the crucial balance between embracing digital advancement and maintaining the ability to adapt and innovate when technology fails. It's a reminder that while technology can enhance efficiency, the core of healthcare remains in human adaptability, empathy, and the unrelenting pursuit of patient well-being, even in the face of unforeseen challenges.

How it Affected Primary Care

The impact of the WannaCry ransomware attack extended deeply into the sphere of primary care within the County Durham and Darlington NHS Foundation Trust (CDDFT).

Primary care providers, often the first point of contact for patients in the healthcare system, were confronted with a series of challenges.

Disruption of Automated Blood Results Transfer

The digital age has made the transfer of critical patient information, such as blood results, a routine and automated process. But when WannaCry struck, it halted the automated transfer of blood results. This disruption put a bottleneck on vital information flow, potentially delaying diagnosis, treatment decisions, and patient care.

In the face of this technological failure, primary care providers reverted to paper, a method slower and less efficient than the automated system. The adaptation, though not ideal, enabled the continued flow of essential information and allowed care providers to make informed decisions.

Limited Access to Case Loads for Certain GPs

Primary care often relies on digital records to track and manage patient care. With the ransomware attack, certain General Practitioners (GPs) found themselves unable to access their caseloads. This situation created confusion, delays, and the risk of reduced continuity of care.

However, the system's resilience became evident as some GPs could access their caseload by navigating through the Urgent Treatment Centers. This maneuver showcased adaptability and a commitment to overcoming barriers to maintain patient care.

Lessons Learned from the WannaCry Attack

The impact on primary care led to carefully examining the existing system and implementing strategies to strengthen resilience. Pathology Business Continuity Plans (BCP) were updated to include specific actions in the event of a future cyberattack.

Primary Care BCPs were also updated to encompass the process of accessing case loads via Trust Urgent Treatment Centers, ensuring that valuable lessons were embedded into future preparedness plans.

The WannaCry ransomware attack's impact on primary care within CDDFT revealed both vulnerabilities and strengths. It exposed the dependence on digital systems and the potential pitfalls when those systems are compromised. Yet, it also unveiled the tenacity, adaptability, and ingenuity within the primary care sector.

Faced with unprecedented challenges, primary care providers adapted quickly and creatively to ensure that patient care continued. The experience was a stark reminder of the importance of a dual approach: embracing the efficiencies of modern technology while maintaining the ability to revert to manual processes when needed.

The lessons learned were not merely theoretical but translated into actionable changes in policies and procedures. These changes not only fortified the response to potential future threats but underscored the central tenet of healthcare: the unswerving commitment to patient well-being, no matter the obstacles.

The story of primary care in the face of WannaCry is a microcosm of a broader narrative about the intersection of technology and healthcare. It's a tale of reliance, resilience, adaptation, and growth that resonates with the evolving healthcare landscape in the digital age. It stands as a testament to the human factor that remains at the heart of medicine, even in an era increasingly defined by technology.

What This Means for You

These organizations didn't just weather the storm—they learned from it. Business Continuity Plans (BCPs) were revised, highlighting the delicate interdependencies within the NHS. Plans were updated to include direct dial numbers, secondary DVDs, and new emergency protocols, reflecting a systemic learning process.

The story of WannaCry's impact on CDDFT is emblematic of our digital era's complexities. It's a lesson in vigilance, adaptability, and interconnectivity. Beyond the immediate response, it underscores the importance of comprehensive planning and unity in defense against unseen digital threats.

The saga culminates in a clarion call to all organizations: the digital world is fraught with perils, and only through preparation, understanding, and a collaborative approach can we hope to stand resilient against future cyber threats.

From Passive to Active Defense

In the increasingly complex and interconnected world of cyberspace, understanding the distinctions between passive and active defense is vital for robust cybersecurity. These two paradigms of cyber defense are likened to a continuum of threat and risk, each serving different purposes and having its own upper and lower limits.

The range of activities does not include hacking back		
Passive Defense Within our own network	**Active Defense** Extends outside our own network	**Offense** Extends to other network
Basic security controls, firewalls, antivirus, patch management, scanning and monitoring; perimeter focused	Technical interactions between a defender and an attacker	Operations that enable defenders to collect intelligence on threat actors and indicators on the internet, as well as other policy tools (sanctions, indictments, trade remedies, that can modify the behavior of malicious actors)	Hacking back and operations intended to disrupt and destroy external networks or information without authorization

Figure 4: Active Cyber Defense Alliance, Strategy Group Call for Views Exposure Draft of the Security Legislation Amendment Bill 2020.

Passive Defense

These are internal measures designed to reduce the likelihood of successful cyberattacks, often realized through firewalls, anti-malware, and intrusion detection systems. While these measures form the bedrock of sound cybersecurity hygiene, they are not sufficient to defend against advanced threats.

Active Defense

This category goes beyond the defender's network, employing tactics such as intelligence gathering, honeypots, tarpits, and botnet takedowns. These tactics are more aggressive and can be effective against sophisticated aggressors. However, they come with inherent risks and legal boundaries, and actions outside the defender's network are often restricted to state-controlled entities such as law enforcement and national security agencies.

A common misconception associates active defense with vigilante actions like hacking back. This notion is incorrect—many elements of active defense, such as beacons and sandboxes,[20] are not only legal but widely accepted and employed. Two main definitions of active defense exist in authoritative texts. The Estonian Definition emphasizes proactive measures, while the U.S. Definition broadens the scope to include technical interactions between defenders and attackers and policy tools like sanctions and indictments.

The concept of active defense has roots in traditional military strategy, emphasizing mobility and intelligence to wear down an attacker. Over time, the application to cyber defense has grown, yet remains confined to the defender's network. Some have argued that active defense should be extended outside the defender's network, but legal

---

[20] Beacons are tracking codes planted to detect file access and transfers. Takedowns involve legally dismantling cybercriminal infrastructure like botnets. A sandbox in cybersecurity refers to an isolated computing environment used to safely execute and analyze files or programs without harming systems or data.

restrictions like the U.S. Computer Fraud and Abuse Act inhibit such activities.

Active defense responses are diverse and range from information sharing, denial, and deception to white-hat ransomware and rescue missions to recover assets. These tools, however, must be wielded with precision, adhering to legal boundaries and recognizing the potential risks and consequences. The message from authoritative figures, such as the chief of the Australian Signals Directorate, underscores the serious legal and ethical considerations surrounding active defense. Private entities contemplating offensive hacking are warned against such actions, as evidenced in prominent media stories.

In conclusion, the multifaceted realm of cyber defense, encompassing both passive and active measures, requires a nuanced understanding, balanced judgment, and meticulous adherence to legal and ethical principles. The challenges posed by sophisticated cyber aggressors necessitate a continual evolution of defensive strategies, always calibrated to manage risks responsibly and within the boundaries of the law. The delicate balance between offense and defense, agility and legality, defines the contemporary cybersecurity landscape, demanding technological prowess and ethical discernment.

In a Nutshell

This chapter provided an overview of cyber risk management, emphasizing the importance of rigorous risk assessment and analysis in developing cybersecurity strategies for your organization.

We explored the conceptual foundations of risk, threat, and vulnerability, highlighting how they interact to shape the security environment. Effective risk management requires systematic identification, evaluation, and control of risks.

The stages of a cyberattack were examined, breaking down the attack lifecycle from preparation and intrusion to active breach. Understanding these stages helps organizations implement appropriate defenses. A case study on the WannaCry ransomware attack further illustrates the impact of cyber threats.

Risk assessment and analysis are explained as broad and focused processes, respectively. Risk assessment creates an overarching plan, while risk analysis dives into the details of each risk. Four key risk landscapes are identified–threats, impacts, controls, and assets. We examined visual tools such as heat maps, which are very useful for simplifying risk communication.

We emphasized balancing quantitative data and qualitative expert judgment in assessing evolving cyber threats. We cautioned against bureaucratic risk assessments that potentially lack flexibility. Concepts like business impact analysis, risk registers, and ROI analysis are highlighted as part of a holistic framework.

We explored the spectrum of cyber defense from passive to active measures. Legal and ethical principles must guide active defense strategies like intelligence gathering and deception. Restraint from vigilante responses is advised.

In summary, Chapter 6 underscores that cyber risk management requires systematic analysis, adaptable planning, visualization tools, qualitative insights, and responsible active defense calibrated to manage risks effectively. This sophisticated approach is essential for security in the complex digital landscape.

Key Messages

- Cybersecurity threats pose major risks to organizations and society, necessitating robust defenses.

- Effective cyber risk management requires a systematic process of risk identification, assessment, analysis, and mitigation.

- Risk analysis involves asset valuation, threat analysis, control evaluation, impact assessment, and risk measurement using methodologies like FAIR.

- Key risk information landscapes include threats, impacts, controls, and assets. Each must be thoroughly understood.

- Risk heat maps are invaluable visualization tools that convey risk levels and priorities.

- Historical data has limits in predicting rare cyber events. Expert judgment provides vital qualitative insights.

- Risk registers catalog risks and mitigation strategies. ROI analysis ensures economic rationality.

- Bureaucratic risk assessments can be rigid and superficial. Agility and adaptability are crucial.

- Business impact analysis examines the financial, reputational, and compliance impacts of incidents.

- Multivariate, indirect costs require reasonable approximations using transparent methodologies.

- The stages of cyberattacks must be understood to implement appropriate defenses.

- Passive defenses like firewalls provide baseline security hygiene.

- Active defenses employ more aggressive intelligence gathering and deception.

- Legal and ethical principles must strictly guide active defense measures.

- Cyber risk management calls for nuance, adaptability, collaboration, and responsible proactive strategies.

Seven

Why Care About Standards?

I n this chapter, we're about to embark on a journey through the landscape of three vital standards that are more than mere technicalities. They are at the heart of cybersecurity, a term that might seem distant or overly complex if you're not immersed in the field. But before you wonder, "Why should I care about standards?" let me assure you the relevance of these standards to your organization is profound.

The importance of cybersecurity standards transcends jargon and technicalities. Compliance isn't merely a box to check—it's a gateway to tangible benefits. By aligning with these standards and ensuring certifications, your organization can potentially unlock reduced insurance premiums. But that's just the tip of the iceberg.

The Three Pillars of Cybersecurity Governance are:

- **IT Governance (ISSO/IEC 38500):** Ensuring that technology is not just an enabler but a strategic partner in achieving your business goals.

- **Information Security Management Systems (ISO/IEC 27001):** Protecting the lifeblood of your business—your information.

- **Automation and Control Systems (ISA/IEC 62443):** Safeguarding the very machinery and processes that keep your business in motion.

The integration of ISO/IEC 38500, ISO/IEC 27001, and ISA/IEC 62443 standards aren't about mere compliance—it's about building a fortress around your organization's cyber infrastructure. It's about creating a resilient, responsive, and strategically aligned system that supports and propels your organizational mission.

ISO/IEC 38500: Sets the direction, ensuring that technology and cybersecurity are aligned with your organizational vision.

ISO/IEC 27001: Operationalizes this direction, translating it into robust security controls that protect your data and intellectual assets.

ISA/IEC 62443: Takes care of the very heartbeat of your operations—the industrial controls that drive your production lines, energy systems, and vital infrastructures.

In essence, these standards are not about layers of abstraction but layers of protection and strategic alignment. They provide a roadmap for cybersecurity that's rooted in the realities and unique needs of your organization, leveraging information technology not just as a tool but as a vital asset that can fuel growth, innovation, and resilience.

The journey through these standards isn't a technical detour—it's a strategic pathway. As we delve deeper, you'll discover that embracing these standards is not about keeping up with regulations—it's about staying ahead in the game.

Together, these standards provide a comprehensive, multi-layered approach to cybersecurity governance, addressing strategic, organizational, and technical levels. Integrating these standards allows for flexibility in addressing specific needs, sectors, and regulatory requirements.

In essence, the collaboration of these three standards allows for a well-rounded and adaptable approach to cybersecurity governance, providing a clear pathway for organizations to align their security practices with their broader business goals and the unique requirements of their industry.

ISO/IEC 38500—IT Governance

Role: Serves as the overarching governance framework for the organization's IT, including cybersecurity.

Focus: Establishes principles and guidelines to ensure that IT supports organizational goals, complies with legal and regulatory requirements, and uses resources responsibly.

Integration Point: Provides the strategic alignment and overarching policies that guide the specific implementation of the other two standards.

The emergence of an IT Governance Standard[21]

In the bustling city of Sydney, on a bright day in January 2005, a gathering marked the launch of the Australian Standard AS 8015. The event brought together key figures, including the Chief Executive of Standards Australia and the Chief Executive of the Australian Institute of Company Directors (AICD). Their speeches were filled with passion and determination as they outlined a new framework for governing Information and Communications Technology. Directors were entrusted with specific responsibilities and tasks linking their long-established duty of managing business risks.

This launch was not merely the result of a whim, but the culmination of frustration from a Chief Information Officer whose attempts to increase the success rate of IT projects in his company had failed. Together with experts under the leadership of Dr. Ed Lewis, they began to unravel the complex weave of IT failures, understanding the negligence given to Information Technology in the boardroom. They saw IT as not merely technology but a crucial element of

---

[21] This section has been summarized from the work of Mark Toomey "Waltzing with the Elephant" (2009) from which I have taken inspiration and guidance.

strategy and business goals, far removed from the confusing jargon of technology specialists.

The problem was clear: discussions were about the supply of IT, not the demand (business requirements). The challenge was to change the way IT was understood and governed.

What emerged was AS8015, a blueprint to ensure that IT use was efficient, effective, and aligned with business objectives. A new model was established, one that embraced not just projects but the reality of day-to-day business dependence on IT.

International recognition followed, with ISO/IEC 38500 announced in 2008, marking a seminal milestone in the journey. Over 20 nations debated, refined, and finally unanimously accepted this new standard. It improved upon AS8015, clarifying the audience, principles, and guidance on good governance practices. However, it maintained its universal applicability by avoiding rigid structures and processes.

ISO/IEC 38500 was not a one-size-fits-all solution but a guide, complementing existing frameworks like CobiT and ITIL, focusing on the demand side of IT use.

It was a turning point in understanding that traditional IT Governance, with its imbalanced focus on supply, had failed to grasp how IT was utilized within organizations. The introduction of ISO/IEC 38500 was a ground-breaking shift, addressing organizational climate, culture, and the critical nature of IT to business. It highlighted that effective governance required more than just following frameworks–it demanded thoughtful consideration of issues, patterns of behavior, and a guidance system that equally addressed demand and supply.

As new standards continue to be developed, the story of IT governance is a reminder that success lies not in technical jargon and supply-driven strategies but in understanding how technology can further business goals, manage risks, and create value. It's about leading with business insight rather than following technology, transforming IT from an esoteric concept into an essential tool for the future. The unanimous acceptance of ISO/IEC 38500 by the voting nations symbolizes a collective realization of this new perspective, paving the way for more effective IT governance.

International Standard ISO/IEC 38500

ISO/IEC 38500 is a seminal document that has moved the conversation about IT governance beyond mere technology and into the realms of organizational behavior, risk management, and strategic alignment. It serves as a complementary tool alongside existing frameworks and is designed to foster thoughtful consideration, risk management, and value maximization in IT use.

ISO/IEC 38500 emphasizes the alignment of IT with organizational goals and the proper evaluation, direction, and monitoring of IT use. Unlike other standards that solely concentrate on supply, it addresses both supply and demand aspects.

ISO/IEC 38500 emerged from Australia's AS 8015, evolving from a national to an international standard in a remarkably short time. This swift global acceptance attests to its utility in addressing long-standing issues like IT project failures. The standard is built on six core principles: Responsibility, Strategy, Acquisition, Performance, Conformance, and Human Behavior, each integral to an effective IT governance framework. These principles are engineered to be universally applicable, avoiding rigidity and allowing for adaptability across various organizational structures and sizes.

Significantly, ISO/IEC 38500 fills a conspicuous gap by shifting the IT governance lens from mere technology supply to a more strategic alignment with business objectives. This alignment ensures that IT initiatives are not only technically sound but also align with the broader goals and strategies of the organization.

When we pivot to cybersecurity, ISO/IEC 38500 serves as a lynchpin that subtly yet substantially influences an organization's cybersecurity strategy. The 'Conformance' principle naturally dovetails with the need for adherence to established cybersecurity standards like ISO/IEC 27001. Meanwhile, the 'Responsibility' and 'Performance' principles explicitly extend governance oversight into cybersecurity, ensuring not only accountability but also the effective deployment of security measures. Human behavior, another core principle, is revealed as a crucial component, often overlooked, in mitigating cybersecurity risks.

The standard's inherent flexibility allows it to be a cornerstone in the governance of not just IT but all organizational cybersecurity efforts. It doesn't replace but enhances and complements cybersecurity frameworks, situating cybersecurity as an integral part of overarching organizational governance.

In essence, ISO/IEC 38500 stands as a pivotal innovation in the realm of IT governance, universally adaptable and robustly comprehensive. While not a cybersecurity standard, its foundational governance principles make it indispensable in shaping an organization's cybersecurity posture. Therefore, ISO/IEC 38500 serves as a governance lodestar, guiding organizations in the effective evaluation, direction, and monitoring of both their IT and cybersecurity initiatives.

ISO/IEC 27001

Role: Focuses on implementing and managing security controls to protect information assets.

Focus: Includes risk management, access controls, incident response, and other core information security functions.

Integration Point: Aligns with the general governance principles in ISO/IEC 38500 and applies them specifically to information security management across the organization. It can be tailored to support specific sector needs, such as industrial controls, where ISA/IEC 62443 comes into play.

Significance of ISO/IEC 27001

In the tumultuous oceans of the information security landscape in the mid-2000s, the currents of hacking, data breaches, and malware posed ever-growing threats to organizations globally. An urgent need emerged for a systematic framework that could defend critical information assets and provide authoritative guidance on information management.

ISO/IEC 27001 arose as that vital beacon of security and governance, crafted through the visionary efforts of esteemed experts seeking to address a worldwide imperative. The development of this standard represented a coordinated international response to the proliferating threats in the digital sphere.

At the helm of this endeavor was Keith Smart,[22] the brilliant chairman who spearheaded the working group that engineered ISO/IEC 27001. His pioneering work in formulating the UK's "Code of Practice for Information Security Management" laid the groundwork for the new standard.

Peter Wood,[23] a tireless champion of computer security, was the catalyst driving the creation of ISO/IEC 27001 in his role as director of the CCSC.[24] Steve North provided

---

[22] Keith Smart is a well-known expert in the field of information security and the ISO 27001 standard. He is the Chief Operating Officer of ISSA-UK.

[23] ISO 27001 Lead Auditor, CEO of First Base Technologies LLP.

[24] Consortium for Computing Sciences in Colleges www.ccsc.org.

invaluable guidance as the leader overseeing the UK government's successful implementation of the standard.

With the publication of its first version in 2005, ISO/IEC 27001 marked a milestone in information security management. Supported by periodic vital revisions in 2013 and 2022, it has demonstrated agility in adapting to an evolving threat climate.

At its core, ISO/IEC 27001 is built on three foundational principles that serve as pillars of information security:

Confidentiality: Safeguarding sensitive information from unauthorized access

Integrity: Ensuring the accuracy and completeness of information

Availability: Guaranteeing access to information when needed

The standard delineates control families that together map out an organization's holistic security posture–from information policy to compliance, and incident response to business continuity. This comprehensive framework empowers organizations to address information risks with rigor.

Globally recognized, ISO/IEC 27001 holds crucial significance for entities across all sectors seeking to fortify their information assets. Its value extends beyond risk reduction to fostering a culture grounded in responsibility and excellence.

With its structured approach, ISO/IEC 27001 provides authoritative guidance to organizations navigating the intricate legal and threat climates of the digital age. Adopting the standard represents a definitive commitment to information security and the foundational principles of confidentiality, integrity, and availability.

SA/IEC 62443

Role: Addresses the specific needs of securing industrial control systems.

Focus: Provides guidelines for securing control systems within industrial environments, such as factories, power plants, and other critical infrastructure.

Integration Point: Works within the broader governance and information security framework provided by ISO/IEC 38500 and ISO/IEC 27001 but focuses specifically on the unique needs and risks of industrial environments.

Industrial Automation and Control Systems Security–SA/IEC 62443

In the complex and ever-evolving landscape of Industrial Automation and Control Systems (IACS), a beacon of guidance shines through the intricacies of cybersecurity, safety, and reliability. It's the ISA/IEC 62443 Series–not merely a collection of standards but a robust framework embodying the collective wisdom and foresight of industry experts.

The ISA/IEC 62443 Series serves as a comprehensive guide to fortifying Industrial Automation and Control Systems (IACS) against cyber threats. It presents a phased approach, beginning with the general group of documents, which lays the theoretical groundwork and introduces key concepts, models, and quantitative metrics. This segment essentially sets the stage for informed decision-making.

The Policies and Procedures segment of IEC 62443 serves as the fundamental blueprint for developing resilient IACS security, offering guidelines for systematic protocol development across vital domains, including risk assessments and patch management. These documents facilitate the evaluation of necessary protection levels and establish governance structures for efficient IACS implementation, enabling industrial operators to build and adapt robust architectures in response to evolving threats.

Next, the System Requirements documents form the architectural backbone for secure systems, outlining specific technological and managerial needs. It serves as a roadmap to build systems capable of withstanding cyber threats effectively.

The Components and Devices documents further fine-tune the security framework at the granular level, focusing on Programmable Logic Controllers (PLCs), Human-Machine Interfaces (HMIs), and network devices. These documents emphasize precision in system components.

The application of the ISA/IEC 62443 Series yields numerous benefits, including robust cyber defenses, standardized approaches for greater collaboration, holistic security measures that evolve over time, and strategic risk management for cost efficiency.

In terms of scope, the ISA/IEC 62443 standards apply to a broad range of IACS used across various industrial sectors.

Examples include:

- SCADA Systems,
- Distributed Control Systems (DCS),
- Programmable Logic Controller (PLC),
- Human Machine Interface (HMI),
- Industrial Robots,
- Building Automation Systems,
- Process Control Systems,
- Safety Instrumented Systems,
- Intelligent Transportation Systems,
- Energy Management Systems,
- Smart Grid Systems,
- Manufacturing Execution Systems,
- Industrial Networking Devices, and
- Industrial Internet of Things (IIoT) devices.

By offering guidance at multiple layers — from general governance to specific devices — ISA/IEC 62443 ensures a cohesive, resilient operation of IACS, making it a foundational asset for industrial cybersecurity.

Certifications for Professionals Working in Cybersecurity

Certifications for ISO/IEC 38500, ISO/IEC 27001, and ISA/IEC 62443 provide assurance that an organization's processes, systems, or individuals meet the specific standards. Here's a brief overview of the certifications available for each:

ISO/IEC 38500—IT Governance

While ISO/IEC 38500 does not have specific individual certifications, organizations can get certified to demonstrate that their IT governance aligns with the principles of the standard. Many certification bodies offer assessment and certification services for this standard.

ISO/IEC 27001—Information Security Management Systems (ISMS)

Organizational Certification: Organizations can obtain certification by implementing an ISMS according to the ISO/IEC 27001 requirements. This certification is often performed by accredited certification bodies, such as BSI, SGS, and others.

Individual Certification: Professionals working in information security can also pursue certifications that align with the standard, such as:

ISO 27001 Lead Auditor: For professionals who want to conduct and lead ISMS certification audits.

ISO 27001 Lead Implementer: For specialists involved in implementing and managing an ISMS.

ISO 27001 Internal Auditor: For those who want to perform internal audits of the ISMS.

ISA/IEC 62443–Industrial Automation and Control Systems Security

Organizational Certification: There are certification programs where products, systems, and services can be certified to the different parts of the ISA/IEC 62443 standard. Organizations like the ISA Secure program or TÜV offer these certifications:

- **Individual Certification:** Professionals working in industrial cybersecurity can obtain certifications such as:

- **ISA/IEC 62443 Cybersecurity Expert (ISCE):** Recognizes individuals who demonstrate a deep knowledge of the ISA/IEC 62443 standards.

- **ISA/IEC 62443 Cybersecurity Fundamentals Specialist:** For those who need a solid understanding of the fundamental principles.

The availability of these certifications may vary by region, and choosing a recognized and accredited certification body or training provider is essential. Certifications not only demonstrate compliance and competence but also contribute to continuous improvement and instill confidence among stakeholders, partners, and customers.

In a Nutshell

Three critical cybersecurity standards—ISO/IEC 38500, ISO/IEC 27001, and IEC/ISA 62443—serve as fundamental building blocks for robust cybersecurity governance. They extend benefits beyond mere compliance, impacting operational costs positively and even offering the possibility of reducing insurance premiums.

Adherence to ISO/IEC 38500 elevates cybersecurity to a strategic priority, counteracting the view that it's merely a technical consideration. ISO/IEC 27001 operationalizes this by implementing robust safeguards for critical information assets. IEC/ISA 62443 focuses on the security of industrial control systems essential for production.

These standards are designed to work in alignment, offering multiple layers of protection tailored to an organization's specific needs and objectives. This multi-layered approach is essential for staying ahead of evolving cybersecurity threats.

ISO/IEC 38500 provides the foundational principles for cybersecurity governance, offering direction and oversight.

ISO/IEC 27001 establishes tangible security controls for information assets. IEC/ISA 62443 targets the secure operation of industrial control systems. Integrated, they extend from executive governance to operational levels, harmonizing business objectives with technological strategy and operational integrity.

The adoption of these standards reflects an industry-wide initiative to address cybersecurity risks. Their integration and certification are not optional but necessary steps for organizations aiming to secure their digital and operational assets in a continually evolving cybersecurity landscape.

Key Messages

- We covered three major cybersecurity standards—ISO/IEC 38500 for IT Governance, ISO/IEC 27001 for Information Security Management Systems (ISMS), and IEC 62443 for Industrial Automation and Control Systems Security.

- We emphasized that these standards provide tangible benefits beyond just compliance, such as reduced insurance premiums, relevant to any organization.

- ISO/IEC 38500 sets the strategic direction to align IT and cybersecurity with business goals. ISO/IEC 27001 focuses on implementing security controls to protect information assets. IEC 62443 deals with securing industrial control systems.

- The standards work together to provide layers of protection, not just abstraction. ISO/IEC 38500 provides an overarching governance framework. ISO/IEC 27001 applies it to information security. IEC 62443 addresses unique industrial control system needs.

- The origins and evolution of ISO/IEC 38500 are covered, stemming from efforts to address IT project failures by improving IT governance.

- ISO/IEC 27001 emerged as a coordinated international response to growing cyber threats in the 2000s. Its principles of confidentiality, integrity, and availability are explained.

- IEC 62443 provides comprehensive guidance on securing industrial automation and control systems, covering different system components and requirements.

- Certification options are outlined for organizations and professionals related to each standard, providing validation of compliance and expertise.

Eight

The Ethics of Cybersecurity

C ybersecurity as a professional discipline has been growing rapidly for decades, with no slowdown in sight. With the growth of the profession of cybersecurity and the bad actors that it is protecting against, ethical considerations have become paramount. Ethical standards and practices in cybersecurity refer to the moral guidelines and principles governing the behavior of individuals and organizations working in the field.

Recap: Cambridge Analytica and Facebook

We introduced this case study back in Chapter 2. The Facebook and Cambridge Analytica scandal began in early 2018, revealing that Cambridge Analytica had improperly obtained personal data from over 87 million Facebook users.

The data was harvested through a quiz app in 2015 and was used to build psychological profiles for political campaigns, including Donald Trump's campaign and Brexit Leave campaigners. Despite Facebook's claims that users knowingly provided their information, the issue led to Congress questioning Facebook, a $5 billion fine from the Federal Trade Commission, and a series of suspensions. Emails also suggested that Facebook might have been aware of Cambridge Analytica's practices as early as September 2015 but failed to act, leading to significant financial and reputational damage.

The scandal also revealed potential Russian connections and underscored the critical importance of data protection and responsible handling of user information.

This, in our opinion, raised a very important *"tug of war"* between making money and 'doing the right thing'. As exemplified by this quote from Nicole Perlroth, Sheera Frankel, and Scott Shane from the Australian Financial Review (March 20, 2018):

> *"One central tension at Facebook has been that of the legal and policy teams versus the security team. The security team generally pushed for more disclosure about how nation states had misused the site, but the legal and policy teams have prioritized business imperatives."*

Do we have the evidence to support our beliefs?

I have a very strong belief in the importance of evidence. This belief didn't just come out of thin air (or my Baptist upbringing). It's something that was sparked by a profound essay, "*The Ethics of Belief*," penned by the Cambridge mathematician and philosopher William Kingdon Clifford. He shared these ideas with the Royal Society in London back in 1877, and it was subsequently published in the journal called Contemporary Review.

Allow me to break down Clifford's argument for you. He doesn't just think it's wrong to believe something without solid evidence–he believes it's morally reprehensible. This isn't about personal preference but a fundamental moral duty to ourselves and others. Our beliefs shape our actions, and if those beliefs are built on shaky ground, they can lead to harmful consequences.

Consider this illustrative story from Clifford's essay: A shipowner sells tickets for a transatlantic voyage, even though on its return from its most recent voyage, the captain informed the shipowner that the ship <u>might</u> not be seaworthy (*might not ... not an absolute*). The ship owner convinces himself that one more journey before undertaking repairs is a reasonable business risk. In one version of Clifford's story, the ship owner collects insurance money when the ship sinks. In another version, the ship makes it safely to its intended destination. The question that is posed in ethics discussions about the Clifford essay is whether the actions of the ship owner were moral, given what he knew before the ship sailed. Was his decision to set sail immoral because the ship sunk in scenario one? Or was it a moral decision in scenario two because the ship arrived at its destination without loss of life—in other words, is the determination of morals based on outcomes or what the ship owner knew or should have known prior to the ship sailing?

Clifford's point is the same in both scenarios: the shipowner is guilty of believing something without sufficient evidence. His sincere belief doesn't excuse his lack of honest investigation. Was it reasonable for the ship's owner to risk the lives of passengers on a journey with a reasonable risk of failure? Did the ship's owner make a reasonable assessment of the ship's safety prior to the final voyage? What evidence did the ship's owner rely upon to make the decision to set sail once more?

Now, in Clifford's telling, this is not just his opinion—he presents it as a universal truth. He famously stated: *"It is wrong always, everywhere, and for anyone to believe anything on insufficient evidence."* Some have found his stance too rigid, like William James, who referred to Clifford as a *"delicious enfant terrible"* and penned his own more permissive view in *"The Will to Believe."*

Yet the lasting impact of Clifford's essay, and what resonates so strongly, is his insistence that we must have reasonable evidence for our beliefs. This means only believing in things when we thoroughly examine the evidence and reasoning behind them. To do otherwise is not only intellectually careless—it is morally wrong. It's a powerful thought, one that has become a cornerstone of discussions on belief and ethics. And I must say, I personally agree with Clifford's standpoint when it comes to cybersecurity.

I assert that Clifford's "Ethics of Belief" can and should be applied to the Cambridge Analytica/Facebook scandal (and other similar cybersecurity breaches), illuminating some of the ethical challenges and considerations in the scenario.

Evidence and Belief

At the core of Clifford's philosophy is the moral duty to believe only what can be substantiated by sufficient evidence. In the context of the Cambridge Analytica scandal, this would place an ethical burden on Facebook to thoroughly investigate any allegations or suspicions about the misuse of data by Cambridge Analytica. Ignoring or suppressing doubts because it was profitable, as the shipowner did in Clifford's story, would not only be intellectually dishonest but morally wrong.

Responsibility for Consequences

Clifford asserts that beliefs influence actions and can lead to real-world consequences. By failing to make themselves fully aware of what Cambridge Analytica was doing with Facebook users 'data and acting upon the knowledge of that data misuse, the decision-makers within Facebook allowed Cambridge Analytica to continue harvesting data, potentially influencing political outcomes. The failure to act responsibly in line with evidence may have contributed to significant societal implications.

Moral Duty to Others

Clifford's principle is not just about personal integrity—it extends to a moral duty to others. Facebook's failure to act on evidence may be viewed as a betrayal of the trust of millions of users who expected their data to be handled responsibly. The ethical responsibility extends to ensuring that actions (or inactions) don't harm others, especially when there is awareness of potential risk.

The Right to Believe

Clifford famously stated that it is wrong to believe anything on insufficient evidence. In the scandal's context, this would include not just Facebook's beliefs about Cambridge Analytica's actions but also the beliefs that users and the broader public might form based on the data and targeted advertising. If these beliefs were shaped by data obtained and used unethically, serious ethical questions about the legitimacy of those beliefs would arise. What was the evidence that Facebook relied upon to enable Cambridge Analytica?

Corporate and Social Ethics

Finally, the application of Clifford's "Ethics of Belief" to this scandal raises broader questions about corporate and social ethics in the age of big data. It underscores the importance of robust ethical guidelines and practices in handling user data and the moral duty that companies have to act responsibly, transparently, and in accordance with the evidence. Your organization is provided with an extraordinary amount of very personal data about your customers and the community. What ethical guidelines do you have in place to ensure that data is not misused? If we follow Clifford, what should we have known about the data with which we are entrusted in the circumstances of that date being hacked or leaked to the public? Should we have known that the data we hold could be misused by bad actors, and are we accountable for that misuse, knowing its potential for abuse?

In summary, Clifford's "Ethics of Belief" provides a framework for understanding the moral failings that were exposed in the Cambridge Analytica/Facebook scandal. It highlights the importance of evidence-based belief and action, the responsibility for the consequences of those beliefs, and the ethical duty that organizations have to their users and the wider society. Applying Clifford's principles to this case underscores the complex ethical landscape of data privacy and the moral imperative for transparency, integrity, and responsibility in our digital age.

By adhering to these and other ethical guidelines, cybersecurity professionals can build trust with clients, colleagues, and the public while also contributing positively to society and the field at large. Ethical conduct is not only a matter of personal integrity but is also crucial for the overall success and credibility of the cybersecurity industry.

Extrapolating from the various international conventions, laws, and standards, we can deduce some key drivers for an organization's journey into the world of cybersecurity:

- **Privacy and Confidentiality:** Respecting and protecting the privacy of individuals, clients, and organizations is paramount. This involves proper handling, storage, and disposal of personal and sensitive information, ensuring that only authorized individuals can access it.

- **Integrity:** Integrity refers to maintaining the accuracy and consistency of data and systems. Altering or manipulating data in unauthorized ways can lead to loss of trust, legal penalties, and other negative consequences.

- **Authorization:** Only accessing systems, networks, or data for which one has explicit permission is a fundamental ethical standard. Hacking into unauthorized areas, even if it's done with good intentions, violates this principle.

- **Compliance with Laws and Regulations:**
  Cybersecurity professionals and the organizations
  they serve must comply with all relevant laws,
  regulations, and international agreements. This
  includes things like data protection regulations,
  intellectual property laws, and export
  controls–especially when it is inconvenient.

- **Professional Competence:** Professionals should
  strive to maintain high levels of competence,
  staying up-to-date with the latest technologies,
  threats, and mitigation strategies. They should also
  refrain from taking on work they're not qualified to
  handle.

- **Conflict of Interest:** Cybersecurity professionals
  must avoid situations where personal interests
  could improperly influence or conflict with
  professional judgment or obligations.

- **Transparency and Disclosure:** Professionals
  should be candid about their actions,
  methodologies, and intentions, which includes
  being forthright with clients about potential risks
  and challenges. Moreover, in cases where a
  vulnerability is identified, ethical responsibility
  dictates that they report it to the owner of the
  affected system or relevant authorities. This
  practice, known as responsible vulnerability
  disclosure, helps preempt any malicious
  exploitation by allowing the timely rectification of
  the identified vulnerabilities.

- **Social Responsibility:** Cybersecurity professionals should consider the wider social implications of their work, including how it might affect human rights, civil liberties, and societal norms.

- **Avoiding Harm:** Minimizing harm to individuals, organizations, and society at large is an overarching ethical consideration. This includes preventing unnecessary disruptions to systems, avoiding collateral damage, and considering the potential negative effects of actions taken.

- **Cooperation and Collaboration:** Cybersecurity is a shared responsibility, and professionals are often encouraged to work together across organizational and national boundaries to address common threats and challenges.

- **Professional Organizations and Codes of Ethics:** Various professional organizations provide codes of ethics that serve as guidelines for cybersecurity professionals and for organizations at large. For example, (ISC)² has a Code of Ethics that its members are expected to adhere to, and ISACA also has a code of professional ethics.

In a Nutshell

The Cambridge Analytica scandal starkly illuminated the complex ethical terrain of the digital landscape, underscoring the profound consequences of unprincipled handling of user data. This egregious breach of public trust catalyzed a broader reckoning on the moral imperatives guiding technology giants and cybersecurity practitioners alike.

At the scandal's core was the startling revelation that the data of over 87 million Facebook users had been improperly harvested and weaponized for targeted political advertising by Cambridge Analytica. Facebook's failure to vigilantly investigate and act upon early warning signs enabled this large-scale data exploitation and manipulation.

When viewed through the lens of philosopher William Kingdon Clifford's seminal "Ethics of Belief," the moral failings in this case come into sharp focus. Clifford forcefully asserted that it is our universal duty to proportion belief to evidence and to diligently consider the consequences of those beliefs on others. Failure to do so is not mere intellectual laziness but a breach of fundamental ethics.

In this context, Facebook's inaction represents a dereliction of its ethical responsibility to thoroughly investigate and halt Cambridge Analytica's misconduct. Turning a blind eye, despite suspicions, violated the duty of care owed to millions of users who entrusted their personal data. The ripple effects of enabling such malevolent data use raise profound questions about social responsibility in the digital age.

For cybersecurity practitioners, Clifford's philosophy highlights the paramount importance of evidence-based action, integrity, competence, transparency, and avoidance of conflicts of interest. It is not simply a matter of personal morality but a professional imperative. Guarding privacy, securing systems, disclosing vulnerabilities ethically, and considering the broader societal impacts of one's work is essential.

Codes of ethics from bodies like (ISC)2 and ISACA provide actionable frameworks. Yet lasting ethical conduct requires internalizing core values like honesty, responsibility, and humility. By embodying such values, cybersecurity experts reinforce public trust and contribute positively to their field.

In an era defined by data's unprecedented power and vulnerabilities, Clifford's 19th-century treatise on ethics rings with new urgency. Its central lesson remains timeless: our duty to the truth, to others, and to the consequences of our beliefs and actions. This applies not just to individuals but also to the corporations wielding society's precious resources. We dismiss such duty at society's peril.

Key Messages

- The Cambridge Analytica/Facebook scandal revealed egregious mishandling of user data and raised profound ethical questions.

- Philosopher William Clifford asserted a universal moral duty to believe only what is supported by sufficient evidence.

- In the context of the scandal, Facebook failed its ethical obligation to thoroughly investigate the misuse of data by Cambridge Analytica despite suspicions.

- Turning a blind eye to available evidence enabled large-scale exploitation of user data, with potential broad societal impacts.

- Clifford emphasizes responsibility for the real-world consequences of our beliefs and actions, including harm to others.

- The scandal highlights the moral duty companies have to act responsibly and transparently with user data.

- For cybersecurity professionals, Clifford's principles underscore the importance of evidence-based action, integrity, competence, responsible disclosure, and social responsibility.

- Adhering to professional codes of ethics and internalizing core values like honesty and accountability are essential for ethical conduct. In the digital age, Clifford's treatise on proportionality of belief to evidence rings with new urgency and relevance.

- Both individuals and corporations have a profound ethical duty to truth, transparency, and responsible use of data that affects society.

Nine

Nutshell of Nutshells

As our world becomes increasingly interconnected through digital technologies, cybersecurity has emerged as a crucial priority for governments, businesses, and society. This book provides executives and managers an accessible guide to the multifaceted landscape of cybersecurity, equipping them with the knowledge needed to govern and make informed decisions.

The book emphasizes that cyberattacks and data breaches are serious threats facing all organizations today. Leaders are responsible for understanding cyber risks and overseeing effective security strategies tailored to their business needs.

We explore the history of cybersecurity, its objectives like confidentiality and system availability, and the inherent challenges in balancing usability and security. Employees can be both guardians and unwitting threats when it comes to cybersecurity.

Numerous frameworks and standards exist to guide cybersecurity programs, controls, and governance. Adherence isn't just about compliance but about building robust defenses and resilience. We outline prominent standards bodies and best practices documents that organizations should align with.

The militarization of cyberspace has led to increasingly sophisticated state and non-state threats. Offensive capabilities raise ethical dilemmas. Information warfare, espionage, and critical infrastructure risks represent growing challenges for both public and private sector entities.

Intellectual property and data have become extremely valuable assets, making cyber theft attractive and potentially disastrous. Supply chain complexity, legal gaps, third-party risks, and insider threats make protecting these digital assets an intricate task.

After exploring the threat landscape, we delve into relevant laws like the U.S. CLOUD Act and EU GDPR, highlighting potential jurisdictional conflicts. International conventions foster cooperation on cybersecurity, cybercrime, and data protection, but achieving consensus remains complex.

We emphasize risk management methodologies that involve asset valuation, threat analysis, security controls, impact assessment, and risk measurement. Techniques like heat maps effectively communicate risks and priorities. Statistics have limits in predicting cyber events, so qualitative insights are indispensable.

Cybersecurity governance requires implementing key standards like ISO 38500, ISO 27001, and IEC 62443. Certification demonstrates alignment and competence. We stress the need to integrate strategic direction, robust information safeguards, and industrial control systems security.

Finally, ethics in cybersecurity entails principles like privacy, integrity, responsible disclosure, and avoiding harm. The Cambridge Analytica scandal revealed the consequences of unprincipled data handling. Upholding ethical duties fosters public trust.

In conclusion, leaders today must embrace cybersecurity as a complex, multifaceted priority. Staying current, asking questions, managing risks responsibly, and governing competently and ethically are fundamental imperatives. Cybersecurity is a continuous journey that demands collaboration, resilience, and vision to navigate the digital frontier.

Key Messages

- Cybersecurity threats like hacking and data breaches are serious risks for all organizations today–large, small, private, public, and government. Leaders of all organizations have a responsibility to understand and oversee effective cybersecurity strategies.

- There are numerous cybersecurity standards and best practices that organizations should align with to build robust defenses beyond just compliance. These include frameworks from ISO, NIST, ISF, and more.

- The increasing militarization and commercialization of cyberspace have led to more sophisticated threats from state and non-state actors. This has raised ethical issues around offensive capabilities.

- Intellectual property and data have become extremely valuable digital assets, making cyber theft enticing. However, protecting these assets is complex due to supply chain risks, legal gaps, etc.

- Relevant laws like the U.S. CLOUD Act and EU GDPR have jurisdictional limitations and conflicts when it comes to cybersecurity and data protection.

- International cooperation is essential, but achieving consensus on cyber norms remains challenging. Conventions aim to foster collaboration on cybercrime, security, and data protection issues.

- Risk management methodologies that use both quantitative and qualitative techniques are indispensable for cybersecurity strategy. Tools like heat maps help prioritize and communicate risks effectively.

- Key standards like ISO 38500, ISO 27001, and IEC 62443 need to be implemented to govern IT, information security, and industrial control systems, respectively.

- Ethics in cybersecurity entails principles like privacy, integrity, responsible disclosure of vulnerabilities, avoiding harm, and considering social impacts.

- Overall, leaders must embrace cybersecurity as an evolving, multifaceted priority requiring continuous learning, risk management, competence, collaboration, and an ethical approach.

Postscript

You got to the end of the book, thank you.

In summary, just let me say that cybersecurity is all about keeping our computer systems and networks safe from theft, damage, or folks who aren't supposed to be snooping around.

It's a big deal now, more than ever, with all the gadgets we use. People can get into all sorts of trouble, like hacking, infecting systems with bad software, and tricking people into revealing secrets (that's what they call social engineering).

Now, if you're running a business or an organization, you've got to be on your toes. That means doing things like putting up virtual barriers, training your team, and keeping an eye on risks. And since the bad guys are always coming up with new tricks, staying current is key.

The history part is fascinating, too. Would you believe it all started back in the 1960s? And now, here we are, dealing with a whole new world of challenges.

But it's not just about keeping our gadgets safe. It's about protecting stuff like personal information and the great ideas that can make or break a business. If something goes wrong, it can cost a fortune, not to mention people may lose faith in you.

And here's the kicker: It never ends. You've got to keep checking, updating, and training. It's like a garden—you've got to keep tending to it.

Let's not forget why this matters so much. It's not just about saving a buck—it's about keeping our customers, colleagues, and even our way of life safe. Quite a task, right?

So, wrapping it up, cybersecurity isn't just a tech thing. It's a living, evolving challenge that affects every part of our lives. It's about protecting not just our gadgets but our identities, money, businesses, and entire way of life. It's big and important, and as the world keeps changing, it's something we all need to be mindful of.

Thank you very much for sticking with me through this journey.

I hope that you have learned some skills that you will be able to apply in your professional and personal lives.

Appendix

Throughout this book, I have endeavored to keep the writing in a style that could be readily understood by executives and managers who need to know about cybersecurity, and others not directly engaged in cybersecurity technical roles, but do not have the time to get buried in technical detail.

Each chapter relied upon quite substantial technical resources.

I offer some sources and references for each chapter here, with additional elaboration, should you want to dig a little deeper.

Chapter 1 References

[1] Von Solms and Van Niekerk, "From information security to cybersecurity", Computers & Security, Vol.38, October 2013, pp 97-102 https://doi.org/10.1016/j.cose.2013.04.004

[2] GGE, U. (2015). Report of the Group of Governmental Experts on Developments in the Field of Information and Telecommunications in the Context of International Security (No. A/70/174). New York: United Nations General Assembly, 1-17.

[3] Jamie Shea, "Cyberspace as a Domain of Operations–What Is NATO's Vision and Strategy?" [https://apps.dtic.mil/dtic/tr/fulltext/u2/1068701.pdf]

[4] Joel R. Reidenberg, 'Lex Informatica: The formulation of Information Policy Rules Through Technology '(1998) Volume 76, Number 3, Texas Law Review.

[5] The UNCITRAL Model law on Electronic Commerce adopted in June 1996, the Model Law on Electronic Signatures adopted in July 2001, and The Convention on the Use of Electronic Communications adopted in November 2005.

[6] United Nations Commission On International Trade Law. (2019). Retrieved from https://uncitral.un.org/

[7] Kubo Mačák, 2016. "Is the international law of cybersecurity in crisis?" In: Nikolaos Pissanidis, Henry Röigas, and Matthijs Veenendaal (editors). 2016 8th International Conference on Cyber Conflict: Cyber Power: 30 May — 03 June 2016, Tallinn, Estonia, pp. 127–139.

Chapter 2 References

[1] http://lca.lawcouncil.asn.au/lawcouncil/cyber-precedent-essentials/cyber-precedent-reality

[2] Four Corners on Cambridge Analytica

The undercover investigation that left social media giant Facebook reeling. We unmask the secretive political consulting firm Cambridge Analytica and the dirty tricks they deployed to undermine the democratic process.

https://www.abc.net.au/4corners/democracy,-data-and-dirty-tricks:-cambridge/9642090

[3] Business Insider magazine, "The Future is Private" Alexandra Ma and Ben Gilbert, August 24th, 2019

https://www.businessinsider.com/cambridge-analytica-a-guide-to-the-trump-linked-data-firm-that-harvested-50-million-facebook-profiles-2018-3

[4] Internet of Things: Are Smart Devices Helping or Harming? | Rose Barker

https://youtu.be/ipdTLJcIkWI

[5] The Journal of Law & Cyber Warfare provides a public peer-reviewed professional forum for the open discussion and education of technology, business, legal, and military professionals concerning the legal issues businesses and governments arising out of cyberattacks or acts of cyberwar. https://www.jlcw.org/

Chapter 3 References

[1] Cybersecurity: Geopolitics, Law and Policy, Amos N Guiora, Rutledge Publishers, New York, 2017, ISBN: 978-1-315-37023-1

[2] "Is the International Law of Cybersecurity in Crisis?", Kubo Macak, 2016 8th International Conference on Cyber Conflict, 2016 NATO CCD COE Publications, Tallinn

[3] "The Cybersecurity Playbook: How Every Leader and Employee Can Contribute to a Culture of Security", Allison Cerra, Publisher: Wiley, September 2019, ISBN: 1119442192

[4] "Effective Cybersecurity: Understanding and Using Standards and Best Practices" William Stallings, Addison-Wesley, NJ, 2019, ISBN-13: 978-0-13-477280-6

[5]   Information   Security   Forum https://www.securityforum.org/tool/the-isfstandardrmationsecurity/

[6] [1] http://www.pewInternet.org/2014/10/29/cyberattacks-likely-to-increase/

[7]https://www.wipo.int/export/sites/www/about-wipo/en/dgo/speeches/pdf/dg_speech_melbourne_2013.pdf

[8] Perloff-Giles, A. (2018). Transnational Cyber Offenses: Overcoming Jurisdictional Challenges. Yale J. Int'l L., 43, 191.

[9] Hanouz, M. D. (2016, October). Understanding Systemic Cyber Risk-Global Agenda Council on Risk and Resilience. In World Economic Forum. Available from: https://www. weforum. org/whitepapers/understanding-systemic-cyber-risk. [http://www3.weforum.org/docs/White_Paper_GAC_Cyber_Resilience_VERSION_2.pdf]

[10] Cornish, W., Llewelyn, D., & Aplin, T. (2003). Intellectual Property: Patents, Copyright, Trade Marks and Allied Rights (6th. London, Sweet & Maxwell)

Chapter 4 References

[1]http://www.uncitral.org/uncitral/en/uncitral_texts.html and https://treaties.un.org/

[2]http://www.uncitral.org/uncitral/en/uncitral_texts_faq.htm
l#model

[3]http://www.uncitral.org/pdf/english/texts/electcom/05-89450_Ebook.pdf

[4]http://www.uncitral.org/pdf/english/texts/electcom/ml-elecsig-e.pdf

[5]http://www.uncitral.org/pdf/english/texts/electcom/06-57452_Ebook.pdf

[6] Nóra Ni Loideain, 'A Bridge too Far? The Investigatory Powers Act 2016 and Human Rights Law 'in Lilian Edwards (ed), Law, Policy and the Internet (Hart Publishing, 2019) 165, 191.

[7] Walker, G. D. Q. (1988). The Rule of Law: foundation of constitutional democracy (Vol. 42). Melbourne: Melbourne University Press.

[8] Hague Journal on the Rule of Law

https://une-edu-primo.hosted.exlibrisgroup.com/primo-explore/search?query=any,contains,Hague%20Journal%20on%2
0the%20Rule%20of%20Law%20&vid=61UNE&search_scope=61
UNE_Search&sortby=rank&tab=61une_search&docid=61UNE_
ALMA5195935870002706&lang=en_U.S.&mode=simple&fromR
edirectFilter=true

[9] Eleni Kosta, 'Communications Data Retention 'in Lilian Edwards (ed), Law, Policy and the Internet (Hart Publishing, 2019) 193, 195.

[10] European Union Agency for Fundamental Rights and Council of Europe, Handbook on European data protection law (Luxembourg: Publications Office of the European Union, 2018) 20.

[11] "AU.S.TRALIA'S 2020 CYBER SECURITY STRATEGY SUBMISSION TO THE DEPARTMENT OF HOME AFFAIRS" EMILY WATSON, GENNA CHURCHES, LYRIA BENNETT MOSES AND MONIKA ZALNIERIUTE 'UNSW Law https://papers.ssrn.com/sol3/papers.cfm?abstract_id=3489650

[12] "A Concise Guide to Various Australian Laws Related to Privacy and Cybersecurity", Srinivas BV., 2020 https://www.sans.org/reading-room/whitepapers/legal/concise-guide-australian-laws-related-privacy-cybersecurity-domains-36072

[13] Australian Regulations related to cybersecurity and data protection:

Sector	Commentary
Banking and Finance	APRA CPG 235 and PPG 234, relevant subsections of RG104 of AFSL licence obligation (RG 104.93 and RG 104.96). Additionally, recommended to follow ISO 27001/2 and COBIT 5
Federal Government	Australian Government Protective Security Policy Framework (PSPF) and Information Security Manual (ISM)
Healthcare Providers	Royal Australian College of General Practitioners (RACGP) Computer and Information Security Standards. National Health and Medical Research Council's "The regulation of health information privacy in Australia". Additionally, recommended to follow ISO 27001/2 and COBIT 5
Internet Service Providers	Communications Alliance C650:2014 icode Australian Communications and Media Authority's "Australian Internet Security Initiative" (ACMA, 2015) Telecommunications (Interception) and Listening Device Amendment Act. Additionally, recommended to follow ISO 27001/2 and COBIT 5

Sector	Commentary
Manufacturing	No specific advice, recommended to follow ISO 27001/2 and COBIT 5
Mining	No specific advice, recommended to follow ISO 27001/2 and COBIT 5
Retailers	No specific advice, recommended to follow ISO 27001/2 and COBIT 5
State Government	Recommended: Australian Government Protective Security Policy Framework (PSPF) and Information Security Manual (ISM) Privacy and Data Protection Act 2014–Victoria Personal Information Protection Act 1998–NSW Privacy and Information Privacy Act 2009–Qld Personal Information Protection Act 2004–Tas Information Privacy Act 2014–ACT Information Act 2002–NT
Telecommunications Providers	Telecommunications (Interception) and Listening Device Amendment Act. Australian Communication and Media Authority's "Australian Internet Security Initiative" ACMA 2015) Recommended to follow ISO 27001/2 and COBIT 5
Utilities	Recommended to follow ISO 27001/2 and COBIT 5

Chapter 6 References

[1]. FAIR–ISO/IEC 27005 Cookbook

[2]. Open Group Standard Risk Analysis (O-RA)

[3]. Technical Guide Requirements for Risk Assessment Methodologies

[4]. Open Group Standard Risk Taxonomy (O-RT), Version 2.0

[5]. Identifying, Analyzing, and Evaluating Cyber Risks Information Security Forum (ISF)

Open Group Standard–Risk Analysis

[1] OAG Risk Analysis pp:8

Index

www.ingramcontent.com/pod-product-compliance
Lightning Source LLC
Chambersburg PA
CBHW071234050326
40690CB00011B/2113